Family Reconstruction

LONG DAY'S JOURNEY INTO LIGHT

Family Reconstruction

LONG DAY'S JOURNEY INTO LIGHT

William F. Nerin

Foreword by Virginia Satir

W · W · NORTON & COMPANY
New York · London

Published simultaneously in Canada by Penguin Books Canada Ltd, 2801 John
Street, Markham, Ontario L3R 1B4

Printed in the United States of America.

First Edition

Library of Congress Cataloging-in-Publication Data

Nerin, William F.
    Family reconstruction.

    "A Norton professional book."
    Bibliography: p.
    Includes index.
    1. Family psychotherapy. 2. Psychotherapy.
3. Psychotherapy patients—Family relationships.
4. Satir, Virginia M. I. Title.
RC488.5.N47   1986   616.89′156   85-15452

ISBN 0-393-70017-8

W. W. Norton & Company, Inc., 500 Fifth Avenue, New York, N.Y. 10110
W. W. Norton & Company Ltd., 37 Great Russell Street, London WC1B 3NU

1 2 3 4 5 6 7 8 9 0

FOREWORD

12 70

Oct, 1986

Because this is the first time that the vehicle, family reconstruction, which I created and developed, is being published in such depth and authored by someone other than myself,[1] I wanted to build a historical and functional frame around it.

Bill Nerin is a former student and currently a colleague. He is a trainer in the Avanta Network Process Community, a nonprofit educational organization which I founded in 1977. This organization is dedicated to assisting the development of becoming more fully human. Family reconstruction, with all it implies, is both a key concept and a philosophy in this training. This is by way of saying that I hold this author in high esteem, as a person, an educator and a practitioner.

This book will be helpful not only to members and students in Avanta Network and those acquainted with my work, but to all those seeking new dimensions to their lives. It is an important first step. It generously and authentically documents the general method, process and outcomes of five reconstructions, one in great detail. I hope that, as we learn more about this powerful and effective tool, there will be many books to follow.

I feel pleased and honored that I have been a midwife to what is turning out to be a very important contribution in

---

[1]*Third Birth*, by Virginia Satir, which includes this material, is now in process.

73562

developing guidelines toward becoming more fully human. By 1965, 20 years ago at this writing, I had developed the rudiments of the procedure and process of family reconstruction. Since that time, I have conducted over 400 reconstructions and have consulted on many more. My work has been seen by many to be an important link to a new consciousness for human beings. Family reconstruction is a concentration of that link. I have done them in many countries and different cultures with many varying symptom manifestations. The results are almost always the same—a significant change in the development of higher self-esteem and responsible taking charge of one's life.

As I continued to use and learn more about this powerful tool, I was also teaching. During the intervening 20 years, people studied with me at different times and for differing periods. Obviously, I could only teach what I knew at the time. What I teach now and what I taught then has greatly expanded. That continues to be true. Family reconstruction is a vehicle that invites the user to continue to explore and learn.

Of course, people took what was available at the time when they were students. They eventually reshaped and adapted the basic concepts to fit specialized situations, adding what they knew to be helpful. For example, Sharon Wegsheider Kruze, author of *Another Chance*[2] and a specialist in the treatment of alcoholic families, calls her adaptation "family restoration." Similarly, while William Nerin clearly labels his work "family reconstruction," he has changed the name of the person having the reconstruction from the "Star" to the "Explorer." When I selected the Star, it was to give support and implicit messages to that person that he/she was in charge of his/her life. The word "Explorer" connotes to me the process of discovering, opening up, and looking at one's life. The designation is different;

---

[2]Science and Behavior Books, 1980.

however, each fits and is positively related to the purpose of the reconstruction.

Family reconstruction did not come as a finished product during a moment of enlightenment. It grew out of both serendipitous and consciously directed happenings, the first of which came when I was five years old. I remember being fascinated, puzzled, and often pained by adult behavior. So much made so little sense. I remember deciding that when I grew up, I would become ''a children's detective on parents.'' Retrospectively, I see that almost everything I have done since that time contributed to my initial goal, that of becoming more fully human. Family reconstruction is a link toward that end.

I do not want to make this into a curriculum vitae. However, I would like to briefly describe enough of my many experiences to shed light on how family reconstruction came to be.

In 1965, when I had developed the form and philosophy of family reconstruction, I had been a professional person for 29 years; six of those years were spent as a public school teacher and principal, and 23 years as a social worker, which included training in graduate school. The conceptual foundation of family reconstruction came from my experiences in pioneering family therapy. My discovery of this form of therapy came as a result of my going into the private practice of social work in Chicago in 1951. The only people available to me then were those that no one else wanted or cared about. The then-current therapeutic approaches had proven ineffective for them. I knew that if I were to be successful, I had to invent something different. The initial families had members who were schizophrenic, criminal or delinquent. Later I saw family members who had psychosomatic difficulties. By the time I had seen 1,400 families (1965), I had seen people that represented a full range of psychological, psychiatric and social disabilities and dysfunctions.

I did find new and successful ways[3] to treat the majority
of these families. These ways came largely through seeing
the operations of these families in the context of self-worth,
communication and system concepts. What had become so
clear in my working with these 1,400 families was how they
used their past to contaminate their present, which in turn
created a future that replicated their past, a stuck place, and
often a hopeless quagmire. The seeds of family reconstruction were sown with this observation.

I reasoned as follows: The past contains the history of
events that have already occurred. It is the *learnings* from
that past that form the approach to the present. To change
the perception and the experience of the present so it can
become a steppingstone to a healthier future, I needed to
somehow introduce ways to stimulate new learnings to take
place. I knew that *new learning is possible.* A person could not
grow another leg or get born at a different time, but he or
she *could* learn something new.

A next step was to create a means of reestablishing the
context in which these old learnings originated and thereby
pave the way for new learnings to happen—"Going back
to old situations with new eyes." These old learnings had
survival significance. This process had to be powerful enough
to allow the surfacing of vulnerability and the development
of new relevant ways to cope.

Old learnings are so powerful because they came at a time
of greatest vulnerability, which also coincided with the time
when there was the least information to judge the usefulness
of what was being learned. This is the time from birth to ap-
proximately age five. Who at this age can make these distinc-
tions? Lacking this ability, the consequences of the time are
integrated as though they were the ultimate truth. For example, if a child interpreted the behavior around him/her

[3]These ways are detailed in my book *Conjoint Family Therapy,* 1964, Science &
Behavior Books, Inc., Palo Alto, CA 94301. Recent additions to my theory and prac-
tice are in *Satir, Step by Step,* coauthored with Michele Baldwin, Science & Behavior
Books, 1984.

as rejecting, as an adult the fear of rejection would be present in forms of rejecting that self or projecting on others. The reasons and contexts might be different, but the same early conclusions would be operative, thus creating the same rejecting reality.

Fortunately, I had the opportunity, during these 23 years, to arrange my life in such a way that I could engage in many pilot projects which continually opened up new possibilities for further exploration. That process continues. I have given myself permission to continue exploration as long as I live. I believe that the last word has not been spoken.

I have already referred to my experience with families in private practice in 1951. In 1955, I joined the faculty of the newly formed Psychiatric Residency Training Program of the Illinois State Psychiatric Institute in Chicago. This exciting and innovative program was largely the vision of a very farsighted man, Dr. Kalmen Gyarfas, a psychiatrist who also headed the program. Dr. Gyarfas believed, first, that mental patients needed to be treated as people, and second, that their behavior needed to be understood in terms of the family system in which they lived. The underlying assumption was that symptomatology was in some way a reflection of the learning imposed by the family system of which the person was a part. The challenge here was to find out how this happened and then to find ways to free the individual concerned so he or she could go on with life.

During my three years with this program, I taught something called Family Dynamics. Teaching forced me to really examine what I was doing and how I was doing it. The Family Life Fact Chronology came out of this experience. This was simply a written chronological account of the events in a person's life within his or her family context. It was neither an anamnesis nor a social history. It was rather more like a biographical chronicle. This vehicle helped me to relate events to patterns of coping over time.

In March 1959, I joined with Don D. Jackson, M.D., and Jules Riskin, M.D., to form the Mental Research Institute in Palo Alto, California. The goal of this institute was to study the relationship of family interaction to health and illness in family members. My contribution was the development of a training program, funded by a private grant. This training experience reinforced my belief that people could significantly change through a "therapeutically oriented educational process." Old learnings were the rules that were developed to help the person survive childhood. If these rules were inconsistent with growth, they would continue to appear in new forms to confound, to paralyze and distort an individual's current life.

Serendipitously, in 1964 I discovered Esalen, where I learned about the affective domain—the world of the inner self. This was related to inner resources of which I never dreamed—altered states of consciousness, LSD, hypnosis, biofeedback, mind visceral learning, mind-body-emotion connections, etc. Gradually I familiarized myself with and integrated this material. I learned a most significant fact through this. I learned that the body, the self, takes in all that happens in its presence from the beginning. Further, the body has ways of deciding which of these experiences will remain in the conscious and which will be sent to the unconscious. Furthermore, I learned there are ways of retrieving unconscious information to help clarify and free a person to learn new ways.

This was a key piece of information. I have since learned how to access relevant information through developing a context of trust and a state of relaxation. This is an initial requirement for effective family reconstruction. What is equally important is that the Guide, the person who conducts the reconstruction, accesses repressed information carefully and gently and with clarity weaves it into new learnings.

The present form of family reconstruction eventually

crystallized in the 30 marathons that I conducted in the years 1964 and 1965.

I am hoping I have conveyed some of the flavor and the significant points in the journey of evolvement toward family reconstruction as it is now. The premises that underlie family reconstruction are what I believe to be basic human realities:

1) Human beings have the inherent capabilities of living productive, joyful lives. The challenge is to access what makes it possible.
2) How human beings cope with the events in their lives is the major factor in determining the outcome of any event.
3) Coping is a process learned during the time when the person was most vulnerable (age birth to five), being at the age when there was the least information to judge the validity and usefulness of what was learned. Since it was an initial learning and came at a time of great vulnerability, it is almost written in blood.
4) Human beings have the capability to divert, suppress, repress, project, deny or distort their natural inherent capabilities to conform to what they perceive to be the demands of survival.
5) At any age, most people can learn new ways of fully thinking and behaving.
6) We are walking manifestations of what we have learned.

When one views human life as sacred, as I do, family reconstruction becomes a spiritual as well as a cognitive experience to free human energy from the shackles of the past, thus paving the way for the evolvement of being more fully human.

A family reconstruction works best when conducted by someone who believes in and reflects the sacredness of life, who recognizes our "cosmic jokery," who leads with heart and soul as well as logic. When we go with heart in addition to head, instead of rigid rules, and when we have a view of exploring instead of presupposing the territory, we will be following the laws of the universe and will discover what our humanness really is.

Virginia Satir
September, 1985

CONTENTS

PREFACE

In 1975 I first experienced family reconstruction in a month-long residential training program conducted by Virginia Satir. I suspected then and am now convinced that family reconstruction is the quickest and most powerful therapeutic process I have ever experienced. It is quick in the sense that the process itself takes about a day to accomplish with the client, whom I call the "Explorer" (Virginia Satir uses "Star"), doing about 10 to 25 hours of homework prior to the day itself.

Since 1975 I have been guiding family reconstructions and teaching others in this method of therapy. While training others and teaching my course in family systems and family reconstruction at the University of Oklahoma, I realized how valuable a book on this subject would be. No thorough treatment of the theory and methodology of this process has been published. Those desirous of guiding family reconstructions might be well served by a handbook setting forth a step-by-step description of the process.

Also, since guiding family reconstructions had taught me more about family systems than anything else, I thought that a book on this subject might offer the readers useful insights about family dynamics. The general populace might gain from this book if I avoided jargon and the scholarly apparatus so often found in professional books. I have tried to do this.

Virginia Satir created family reconstruction between 1965 and 1970. I believe that family reconstruction is the epitome of her work and contribution to the field of family therapy. Virginia brought together in this process elements of gestalt, communications, psychodrama, body work (sculpting), hypnosis, accessing the unconscious, and fantasy—all under the theoretical framework of systems theory and under the operational framework of nurturance and unconditional love. To me it is the exquisite expression of Virginia Satir's genius and loving care for others. I am grateful to her for all that she has given to me by way of teaching and modeling, and in our personal friendship.

As I write these words I feel a tender sense of pride well up in me in being able to share this aspect of Virginia Satir's work and my incorporation of it with others. I believe so strongly in family reconstruction that I feel a sense of achievement in helping to spread its use. I am delighted that those who are not therapists who read the manuscript before publication derived so many personal insights for their own family life. It assures me that, indeed, while this book addresses itself to helping professionals guide family reconstructions, it can help the average person improve his or her family relationships.

A NOTE ON LANGUAGE

I would like to add a comment about my language usage. In writing this book, I found myself torn by my growing sensitivity to the injustice of male chauvinism and the limitations of the English language. When using a third person singular pronoun in referring to a previous noun, should I use he/she, s/he, she/he, or pluralize it by using "they" rather than the singular noun? Personally, I am so accustomed to seeing "he" used as the common word of reference that I find attempts to equalize the male and female gender jarring, and I often must reread the sentence.

The Latin language uses the words "vir" for a male person, "femina" for a female person, and "homo" for a person in general, regardless of maleness or femaleness. Would that the English language were so rich! I have tried my best to avoid the chauvinism of using only "he." However, I have failed to bring it off perfectly. I trust the reader will appreciate the spirit behind my effort and bear with my failure.

ACKNOWLEDGMENTS

I want to acknowledge, again, my gratitude, affection and respect to my good friend and teacher, Virginia Satir, a pioneer in family therapy who years ago used her creative ingenuity to develop this process of family reconstruction; to Lorna Cunkle and Liz Jeep, who offered valuable editorial insights; to Susan Barrows, a most easy editor to work with.

I also acknowledge my debt of gratitude to Gandhi and to Martin Luther King; they are modern examples of people who struggled to incorporate Jesus's way of dealing with threat in a nonviolent, congruent way. They exemplified the paradoxical ways to relate to others so that life is nurtured rather than destroyed.

I also thank my family and my extended family of long and trusted friends in whose company I have somehow learned and experienced love, trust and the courage to give of myself, conquering much personal fear. Finally, I touchingly thank my wife Anne, in whose presence all my previous experience of love and trust finds expression, encouragement and growth. She encouraged and sustained me in the effort of writing this book.

Family Reconstruction

LONG DAY'S JOURNEY INTO LIGHT

1 THE LIGHT OF FOUR EXPLORERS

In the summer of 1975 I spent a month in Banff, Canada, being trained by Virginia Satir in family therapy. During this intensive training I learned about family reconstruction. Family reconstruction seemed to encapsulate and epitomize Virginia Satir's work as a pioneer in family therapy.

Late in that month's training period I said to one of the trainees, "Sandra, all through this month I have been struck by how much you remind me of my sister, Celeste. When I was a kid she used to tuck me into bed every night [Celeste was 14 years older than I]. Those were very special moments for me."

Sandra suggested that we recreate the scene just to see what might happen. So we did. She gently sat on the edge of my bed and tucked me in much as Celeste did. Old memories immediately came back to me! In no more than ten minutes I was overwhelmed with how much Celeste meant to me, how over the previous eight years we had had no special times of being close, and how I wanted to reconnect with her in an intimate way. I resolved to see her in Indiana before the year was up. Late that fall I traveled to her home and spent several quiet days with her, filling her in with all that had been going on with me during the previous ten years. I left Indiana basking in the warmth of having shared myself with her and received her understanding, acceptance and good will. She was always one of the most understanding and accepting persons I ever met. How

3

fortunate and grateful I was to have had that renewed intimacy with her, as she died five years later.

That ten-minute "mini" reconstruction with Sandra convinced me of the power of family reconstruction. It was just one of many scenes that a person might go through in an all-day reconstruction. If that could happen in ten minutes and produce such rewards, what might an entire family reconstruction be like!

It is no small wonder that Virginia Satir developed this process. As early as 1964 she wrote in *Conjoint Family Therapy*, "I make use of principles and ideas gleaned from the disciplines of dance, drama, religion, medicine, communication, education, speech, the behavior sciences, even the physical sciences, from which the 'systems concept' (on which my practice is based) first derived."[1] Being open to such diverse human resources, her genius allowed her to combine Gestalt, psychodrama, body sculpting, fantasy and hypnotic techniques into a marvelous whole guided by the principles of family systems theory.

According to the theory of family systems, since we are the product of and live within a family, the individual must be viewed as a member of that system and therefore, as family therapists, we must treat the system itself. The classical dramatic example of this is the case of a young boy going to a therapeutic residential school, getting better, returning home, and soon reverting to his old unruly behavior. The family system had a major influence upon the actions of the boy. If the family as a whole had been dealt with and changed, then the boy would have returned to a new system supportive of his improved behavior.

Family therapy is an approach that recognizes and deals with this fact. Thus, practitioners of this kind of therapy deal with the family as a whole, either actually or symbolically.

---

[1]Virginia Satir, *Conjoint Family Therapy* (Palo Alto, CA: Science & Behavior Books, Inc., 1967), p. 179.

They see the pertinent members of a family, as well as the so-called "identified patient." Recognition is given to the fact that something is going amiss within the system, not just within one person. Family reconstruction is one of many approaches dealing with this phenomenon.

I view family therapy as having two aspects. The first deals with the members of the client's current family: mother, father, children and any other significant relatives. The second deals with the client's family of origin, going back two or three generations, as seems appropriate. When I deal with the current family, I am dealing with the way mother and father are employing what each of them learned from their family of origin. The current family is the here-and-now expression of those previous learnings and transformed learnings received from one's family of origin. The current family is the expression of how those previous learnings are being blended and imported to the children.

When I deal with a client's family of origin, I am dealing with the way rules, meanings, coping mechanisms and communication patterns were handed on from one generation to another. In dealing with the family of origin, I am going back to the point where dysfunctional patterns were powerfully implanted in a current mother, father or individual adult. What I find so often is that in dealing with a current family, I need to go back to the family of origin to help the adults free themselves from some pattern that is causing trouble in the current family.

When family therapy deals with the family of origin, family reconstruction comes in. Family reconstruction deals with a mother's family of origin, for instance, in such a way that the mother comes away from the therapeutic experience with a new construction of her family of origin. This does not mean that the family of origin is changed or that the mother is raised by a different family through some sort of hypnotic regression. It means that the mother is allowed to see, feel and experience realities of the family of origin *that as a child that mother could not experience!* In this sense, the mother does have a *new* experience of her family as if she were being raised by a different family! This new experience allows for an explosion of old dysfunctional implanted dynamics so that functional dynamics can emerge. It is like a jar containing wine and vinegar salad dressing. If you just pour it on the salad without shaking it, you only get one substance; if you shake it (explode it), you pour a rich mixture of both wine and oil. The shaking transforms the dressing so it is very tasty. Family reconstruction shakes things up so one-sided impressions and dynamics are transformed into a rich mixture of the full reality, leading to a tasty way to live. To accomplish this, psychodrama is used to reenact crucial scenes from the paternal, maternal and immediate family of origin.

However, in doing a family reconstruction we are not treating the actual members of a family in person. We treat the system and the members in it through the use of people playing the roles of the actual family members. There are advantages to this that are not present when seeing the members in person, just as there are other advantages present when treating the real live members.

Treating the family symbolically through the use of role players offers these advantages:

1) The person doing his or her family reconstruction can be more direct, open and emotional with a role player than with the actual family member. The presence of the real parent, for example, may threaten the one (whom I call the Explorer) doing his or her reconstruction. Being so intimidated, the Explorer may freeze in his thinking, insights and self-expression. For breakthroughs to occur, it is necessary to be free to see and deal with what is there—at least within the perception of the Explorer. And indeed, it is the Explorer's perception of reality that determines his reactions, not necessarily the reality itself.

2) Role players, not being entrenched in the psychological

state of the persons they play, are better able to get in touch with feelings, thoughts, desires and propensities that may be present in those real family members but which are hidden from the Explorer. It is crucial for the Explorer to discover those hidden parts of his family member if the Explorer is to change.

3) Role players, of course, can play the roles of those not able to be present.

4) Through role players we can set up the Explorer's immediate family of origin as well as the maternal and paternal families. From these families the mother and father learned the behaviors that they bring together into a marriage that gives birth and rearing to the Explorer. This is critical in enabling the Explorer to see the patterns handed on from one generation to the next and how that was done. This has a powerful impact and helps motivate the Explorer to change.

When guiding a person through a family reconstruction, I see myself going off on a mysterious and adventuresome day's journey, a journey that more often than not leads one into light, a light not previously seen by the Explorer. The light opens up for the Explorer new ways of seeing, feeling, experiencing and *being* that bring a sense of greater congruence with self, family and friends. I hope that in reading this book you can enjoy some of that adventure, too. The names of the people described in this book are fictitious. Their words are factual and their story lines are true.

I have asked four persons whose reconstructions I guided to write their accounts of the experience and what followed thereafter. I introduce each account with some background to aid your understanding.

CHRIS

I had been seeing 28-year-old Chris in therapy off and on for more than a year. We were dealing with his desire to be more assertive with women, his feelings of rejection and loneliness, his fear of being out of town by himself, and his anxiety over an ulcer that would periodically raise its powerful head. Chris was somewhat cautious concerning therapy, getting quick relief from eruptions of pain and then relaxing out of the sessions until the next eruption occurred. Finally, he was frightened by a particularly severe flare-up of the ulcer and committed himself to getting to the bottom of all of this, thus becoming assertive in this very decision. I recommended he get into a family reconstruction group that was being formed, so he did.

Chris knew more about his mother and her side of the family than he did about his father and his family. Chris was very close to his mother, whom he idealized beyond reality. He knew that his mother's mother, now dead, was a very special grandmother to him and he loved her very much. As with most of us, the images he carried around of his mother and his father were rather simplistic, devoid of the subtleties that make up the human personality.

As the reconstruction unfolded, Chris began to see how his father, Jack, was shy and unable to show certain kinds of vulnerable feelings. Jack had come from a farm family; Jack's father was a hard worker and a stoic who exhibited neither affection nor vulnerable feelings. Chris sculpted[2] his father's family with each person doing his or her work and no one touching anyone else.

Chris's mother, Irene, grew up in a big city. Her father, Charles, was a successful and socially prominent financier. Irene's mother, Gladys, didn't have the close and affectionate relationship she wanted with her successful husband, and so she busied herself with social life and looked to her daughter Irene for emotional support and intimacy.

---

[2]Sculpting is a procedure wherein the Explorer puts role players of a family into physical positions as if they were sculpted from blocks of marble. The sculpture can represent either how the Explorer perceives the family or how he or she would like to have seen the family, depending upon the direction of the Guide of the family reconstruction.

Gladys was so confident of her relationship to Irene that she did not feel threatened when Irene married Jack. And as Irene in turn failed to get affection from her shy and inept husband, she turned to her children for intimacy, just as her mother Gladys had turned to her. Jack became a successful businessman, like Irene's father, and their marriage resembled that of Gladys and Charles.

However, when Chris was born, Gladys moved in to get her needs met by this adorable little grandson, spending most of her time in the home of Irene and Jack. Irene went into hidden competition with Gladys over Chris's love and affection. Chris was never conscious of this in his life, but unconsciously he lived obediently to make Gladys and Irene happy. The rule of survival given to him by these two powerful women was: "If you don't make me happy, I'll die."

Chris enjoyed the attention and bounty of both Gladys and Irene while doing all they wanted of him. As a result, he was never in touch with his own unique wants, and he never learned to be assertive, particularly with women. His needs and wants coincided with Irene's and Gladys's; his selfhood was never clearly defined. During his family reconstruction, Chris saw this for the first time. He also had the opportunity to grieve and cry at Gladys's reconstructed funeral—and later, as you will see, he spent 45 minutes crying at home over this loss. The unfinished business of Gladys's death was brought to an appropriate close.

During the family reconstruction, Chris didn't show much emotion, except the tears over Gladys. But underneath his stoic self, powerful feelings were being loosened. Chris went home as exhausted as if he had been emoting all day long. The following is part of the diary I asked him to keep in order to track his experiences after the family reconstruction.

3/12 [The night of the Reconstruction]
One of the funniest days I've had in years. Absorbed in a kind

of fantasy, yet believable portrayal of my family. It was amazing how little I knew or had thought about my family—amazing.

Going into this I was pretty apprehensive. I still have trouble with the notion that unveiling your past will help today's problems. I've always leaned toward forgetting the past; work-from-today type of approach to life. I also didn't think my life could take up a full day's session. (I'm not that significant.) I felt as though I would be boring to the other members of the group, and therefore should try to rush through it. Well, once we got going I felt everyone was enjoying it, and I was so engrossed myself I didn't care what they thought. The day just flew by.

It was unbelievable how all the roles came out just as I imagined them to. *Everything* they did made sense and the only time it didn't was only because I didn't want it to. I didn't want to look at my mother and her mom in a negative way. That was a very upsetting scene.

It felt good to cry. I was kind of embarrassed—not too much. I probably could have cried more.

When the session was over I felt very good but had a million questions. I felt very good all evening. Woke up four o'clock in the morning crying—cried for about 45 minutes, hard. It was a happy cry, thinking of Gladys. Kind of finishing what happened in the session.

3/13

I felt pretty good today, pretty strong, like I was the center of attention and important but a little lonely. Margie [his former girlfriend] came over last night; I had a strong desire to see her today. We talked about us and our breakup. I'm not sure if I called her because I was lonely or just to clear the air with her. I think both. A lot of scrambled thoughts ran through my head all day, sad and joyful. I listened to parts of the tapes, somewhat questioning it (the family reconstruction)—was that really the way things were? I didn't want to find out it was wrong. I didn't want my mother to tell me I wasn't Gladys's favorite, or that my dad really just hated to hunt and fish. I was being too analytical—kind of skeptical although I knew they were probably correct in their roles. I was unsure what it all meant. Was I supposed to be a new person now?

3/14
Felt very lonely today, very confused and it kind of upset me. I didn't understand a lot of my thoughts, feelings, etc. How was I to use this experience? I felt it was a very powerful one indeed and maybe I thought I would be a new person. Was I analyzing it too much? Maybe I thought that all my problems would be solved. Now I realize my mom and grandmother protected me and mothered me but *today I wanted that same thing again from everybody.* I was disappointed in myself. I could have used a follow-up session—I think it would have been very important. There were just too many questions, puzzles, confusion, and I needed to sort them out. What good did the session do? I needed help assimilating all my feelings.

3/16
I felt nauseated for a few days, my stomach kind of upset. I went through a kind of self-pity stage these next few days, feeling I don't have any friends, feeling nobody calls on me, etc. Instead of getting out myself, I just felt sorry for myself.

3/20
Have been missing Margie lately, I think as a friend mostly. I also have been assuming she's been with this other guy a lot. It upset me quite a bit. I called her about seven—he's over at her house along with a bunch of other people. I feel lonely, like I'm missing out on something, maybe jealous. I end up calling her back again that night, let her know I'm kind of upset, talk about our breakup. This is the first time I've done this since we broke up— that is, get lonely and depressed, then call her. I've always sworn I would not call her during a depression. I don't want to lead her on and I don't want to give her false hope.

3/22
Felt good the rest of the week, strong, confident.

3/25
Went to see my barber, who I think is very cute. Got a date with her and feel good.

3/27
Great days.

3/28
Great days.

4/1
Saw Bill Nerin today, he seems encouraged by my progress—made me feel very good, very positive. As I have said before, I'm not sure how to expect change within myself. Now am I getting better? How do I know? What do I look for? I think after my reconstruction, I expected an immediate progression, or change. But I must be patient. It doesn't happen over night. I had some bad days after my reconstruction and it disappointed me very much, but to my surprise it did *not* disappoint Bill. How naive or unperceptive of me to think I won't continue to struggle for some time. I realize that now I'm willing to give myself time to change. It really helped to hear encouraging words from Bill. There were times the last week I thought the reconstruction had failed—not that I have expected that much from it in the first place—but I believe I even felt that I had failed Bill, as if he would be disappointed that I had not had great days since the reconstruction. Well, he thought I was doing very good, showing improvement and I really needed to hear this, not that I always need this sort of support, but at this time in the midst of my confusion about the reconstruction, I needed it and it was *very* important.

[Chris goes into a long description of his past bouts with ulcers, his tight face and grinding teeth, and his being scared to death. Then he continues.]

4/10
For the last month I have had very little stomach problems, none the last two weeks. I slept well, I've eaten well, I started getting out more. My facial tension is gone and I had a date last weekend. Before, I would not ask someone out because 1) my stomach might be hurting; 2) I'd be no fun—depressed; 3) I would get too nervous and therefore create an ulcer. Well, I was nervous, my stomach did not hurt, I was fun, and it was fun. I have not taken

Tagamet in one month. I'm still kind of scared of the new situations as on a vacation or a new job. I still try to keep my life very patterned—not anything out of the ordinary. But I feel reborn, maybe a second chance. I am very positive about my future, but I still worry about my stomach. What if it acts up again? I can't go through that again.

4/15
My facial tension tightened up today a little. I saw Cary, a good friend of Margie and mine who has recently married. She went from an insecure, *lonely* gal to a happy gal since she married. She used to call often, come by often—I used to be her best friend. We needed each other. Now she doesn't need me. I never talk to her anymore and I know I have a lot of feelings building inside of me. I'm sure this had something to do with my tension, but I'm not sure why. It was fun seeing her. Maybe it was seeing her so carefree, so unsympathetic now that she has what she wanted—a husband.

I think I'm going to have to find a new job soon, there's not much work with my company. This thought scares me, a new situation. How will I react physically? I'm not sure I'm ready for it, but then again I look forward to it.

Chris is still making his personal journey of progress, gradually maturing and remaining free of any ulcer recurrence.

ANDREA

I guided Andrea's family reconstruction over eight years ago. She was 34 years old then. Andrea, who perceived her mother as very nonaccepting of her, was struggling with her self-esteem, which was obviously connected to her relationship with her mother. Andrea was so upset about this that she was willing to risk doing her family reconstruction even though she could not know what would ensue. She asked some of her friends to form the group for the day. This in itself showed Andrea's strength. She would lay bare her life before her friends. It was also a tribute to the quality of her friends that she could so trust them.

The following is Andrea's account:

In 1975 I was 34 years old, living with my husband and two children in Oklahoma City. My widowed mother and 39-year-old brother lived in my childhood home in Detroit, Michigan. Another brother, 30 years old and married, lived in a Detroit suburb.

Despite the hundreds of miles between us, a negative relationship between my mother and myself hung over me like a cloud that occasionally rained heavy on my life. In my eyes my mother was my chief critic and there was little I could do to satisfy her.

An especially devastating incident occurred in the spring of 1974. My mother was recovering from pneumonia and a broken arm. My recollection is that I called her long distance (a rare occurrence in our family), feeling somewhat guilty for not having written recently. What followed was a solid hour of her screaming at me. I was ''not concerned about'' her, or I ''would have written more often.'' I heard every aspect of her ill health and of her anger at opinions on moral issues expressed by church members in our newsletter (up until that time I had had our church newsletter mailed to her). I believe it is significant that although I held the telephone away from my ear for much of my mother's diatribe, I could not hang up on her. I did not want to give her one more reason to criticize me.

From that time until my reconstruction, I was a cold, angry, but dutiful daughter. Our relationship increasingly became a yoke around my neck. Mother's Day became a day of bitterness. I was angry at her for not accepting me as I was and blamed her, in part, for my struggle for my own self-acceptance. My request for a family reconstruction stemmed from my desire to discard the yoke effect my mother had on me.

The five-hour reconstruction not only had the immediate effect of freeing me from that yoke, but also has led to an eight-year-long evolution of a positive, warm relationship with my mother.

During the process of reconstruction I realized unequivocally that the actions of my mother (and father) that I perceived as destructive to me were *not* done with the intent of hurting me. Rather, they were actions of human beings who were simply doing the best that they knew how to do, and that the "best" was adversely affecting me during times of stress.

My father's tendency to escape (he used to leave our family for a day or two, and when I was 12 he left our home permanently) and my mother's tendency to criticize or get emotionally or physically ill were the only ways they knew to survive in time of crisis. That realization engulfed me and allowed me to forgive them and shed the burden of bitterness and anger.

My relationship with my mother is now mutually warm and accepting. I have never mentioned the reconstruction to her, but I have wondered why both of us seemed to change. My guess is that she had gone too far. (My brother commented regarding the call that mother felt "she had blown it.") Second, the reconstruction enabled me to hear mother without past defensiveness and feelings of being "attacked." Perhaps unconsciously she realized a change in me—that I accepted her as she was—which, in turn, allowed her to be more accepting of me.

The description of the shift in attitude from Andrea not accepting mother's anger and disapproval to accepting her as she is sounds terribly simple. Why not simply tell Andrea to do that? Why wouldn't Andrea make that simple switch at my suggestion? Because my mere words do not have that power! Andrea had been telling herself to do the very same thing for years. It took the dynamic process of her five-hour family reconstruction to unlock her rigid response to her mother, thereby enabling her to do emotionally and psychologically what she knew in her mind all along. It is one thing to have a new idea and a vastly different thing to have a new integrated psychological state wherein one's emotions, decisions, acceptance and frame of being coincide with the naked idea. For years Andrea had the desire to be more accepting of her mother. "I should not feel this yoke," she constantly told herself. "I shall not be bothered by my mother's anger and criticism." Yet she could not change her behavior. The idea was there; the total psychological state was not. Through the power of the family reconstruction, Andrea achieved her new way of being.

LINDA

I first met Linda when she was a student in one of my classes on family systems. She kept in contact with me, and over several years did two family reconstructions about a year apart. She wanted a second one because she felt she got so much from the first, had worked on the material unearthed from it, consolidated it, and was now open and ready for further progress. I asked her to summarize her experience for me.

My first family reconstruction was in 1982, one and a half years ago, in which my focus was on my fear of being crazy. In the spring of '72 I was admitted to a psychiatric hospital, labeled obsessive-compulsive paranoid schizophrenic, and administered heavy doses of major tranquilizers. After five years, I finally left and told myself I would never, ever let any therapist get that close to me again. Then, when I was introduced to Bill in the process of family reconstruction, I felt a hope and trust deeper than I had felt in a long, long time.

Within my experience of reconstructing my family, seeds of understanding and acceptance began to grow. I began seeing how imprisoned all of my family and I were by the confining, deadening walls we each had fearfully constructed. I began seeing the unconscious inhuman rules that my family and I were defeatingly attempting to follow. As an example of these inhuman rules, I'll share an exchange which transpired between myself, my alter ego, and the woman who played the role of my mother. As I was talking with my "mother," Bill asked me what I was feeling and I replied, "Okay, I guess." He asked me again to get in touch with how I was feeling and I once again was unable to. Then Bill asked my alter ego to step in. She began expressing the anger she was feeling. It wasn't until my alter ego began expressing her anger that I too got in touch with my anger. It was not until that moment that I learned I was living by an impossible set of rules, one being to never express anger. This began to make sense of my ulcer, which I had had while in high school. At that time I was not even aware of feeling anger, much less expressing anger, and so my anger found relief through eating a hole in my intestines.

I reconstructed my family again one year after my first reconstruction. I had invited a friend whom I had not been in contact with for close to a year. This friend represented to me my "crazy" part. In choosing my alter ego I felt a lot of turmoil inside. I chose a person, then I chose Bobbie (my "crazy" friend), and then another person, and then back to Bobbie. At one point Bobbie and I talked, which I hated, and I wanted to make her go away. I wished inside that I had never asked her to come.

I became quite confused, my words became more and more garbled, and eventually I became quite frightened. Then at some point something real exciting happened. I suddenly realized that what I was trying to do was an attempt to avoid my "crazy" friend Bobbie. I was wanting to disown that part of me as if it had never existed—as with my past experiences with camp fires. In attempting to put the fire out by blowing it out, I was only feeding the fire and so creating more flames. I realized that only through accepting that part of me which I defined as "crazy," instead of attempting to blow it out or run from it, could it then be transformed. I realized that a long time ago, with the resources I had at the time, I created that part of me because I needed it. At the time that part of me was my friend and now I did not need that part of me in the same way I had previously, so I could approach the beauty of my old part, thank that part of me and then ask it to grow with me.

As I take more steps I experience some storms, and at times I walk in the dark and I fall into holes, but I have found that I can now use my many treasures within me and can again stand up and with each fall I then walk taller and freer than I had ever before dreamed possible.

Linda has continued in my family reconstruction group. As she plays roles in other people's family reconstructions, she is uncovering more and more of herself, seeing parts not seen before. This is not surprising, as she has had to cover up much of herself in her struggle to survive the ordeal of her early life and consequent institutionalization. Within the trusting environment of therapy and the family reconstruction group, she is slowly unfolding, allowing herself to take one step at a time in her journey into maturity.

DIANA

Diana was part of an ongoing family reconstruction group that met each month for a day, allowing each person in the group to do his or her family reconstruction. Diana, like Linda, had two reconstructions about a year apart. In her story she describes what went on during the family reconstruction.

My first family reconstruction was in the spring of 1982. I say first because I was so emotionally exhausted, emptied, that we [Bill Nerin and the group with me] only reconstructed my father's side for six hours; so much surfaced that I didn't want to go any further in that one day. I think the group would have gone on—as there seems to be endless energy from those who give their day to another person's life and her story with reverence—but I was pooped.

Let me explain. Bill had me construct my father's teenage years, and through that I got in touch with his loneliness and inability to share with anyone except possibly his mother. So, being sensitive to that and to my father as a human being, we moved into his mother's death.

Now let me explain. I had stayed away from funerals as much as possible up to the time of this first family reconstruction. Bill had me reconstruct a scene from the funeral and I shut down. I mean I closed up, went blank, turned away, crossed my arms and tears began to flow. Bill said, "What is it?" I was caught in a dark spot in my mind with the light creeping through so I let another human into my history, a place in my history that was dark and I couldn't turn the lights on by myself. I *needed* another human to go with me to my dark space, my blank space, because I was too afraid to go alone. I *needed* another human who had the courage, not the knowledge of my experience but the courage to go into my fear with me and allow *me* to change it to truth.

This is where I need to tell the reconciliation that takes place. The one person, namely Bill Nerin, with the energy and strength from others, the family reconstruction group, could go with me to a place in me that I hadn't made my own, reconciled it to me. I wanted to go there, not knowing what it was—like the lost sheep within me—my God was leaving the flock for a short while to search out and find and bring back to the fold the lost one, thus making me *whole* with the flock and no longer separated from the rest of me, the community.

My father had sex with me at some point during my grand-mother's funeral. We were in her house, he was crying, no one was comforting him. I was a teenager just developing. He and I had always been close. In a rocking chair he sat crying and lone-ly. I crawled into his lap, wanting to console and becoming too big to do so and having no idea of the sexuality of a man. He fondled me—now fondling, used to be hugging—interesting how fathers and daughters change from being hugged to fondling because of physical changes. My mother, who appropriately should have been there and never could care for Dad this way, was gone. The house was empty and Dad had sex with me. Then made me *swear* never to tell and stayed away from me except at later times when he would fondle me again. I was crushed, my father was *terribly* guilty and our relationship was *dramatically* changed, to say the least. From that day on I blocked this event out of my mind to heal myself. The only sadness there is in block-ing to protect is I blocked many good things from me.

My father went to chemical dependency as he grew older. My father and I quit talking. Crazy things happened around money issues, my parents fought physically, and my father tried to ex-press his ways of love with gifts, money and fondling when he was drunk, but never with a verbal "I love you" or just discus-sions or anything that would make rational or real sense. Thus, I learned to relate to men with nonverbal signals which, as we all know, lead to protection, misunderstanding and tremendous assumptions. By the end of that first day of my family reconstruc-tion I had cried so much and talked so much I felt totally emptied.

Another remembrance of my grandmother's funeral: I prom-

ised my father I would never leave him. So how powerful is a
promise of a young child who has just had sex with her saddened
father at her grandmother's funeral? It is tremendously powerful. So powerful that it would take an equal power to break it. I
found that power sharing it with others in the safe and trusting
environment of the family reconstruction. Within the family reconstruction group there is enough love and care brought by
searching individuals trying to live healthy lives to support my
new way of trying to be.

A year passed before I did my mother's side of my family
reconstruction—time to let forgiveness between my father and me
in a spiritual sense build and go out—pebbles causing waves. I
did my mother's side of the family reconstruction on another day
because of the exhausting effects of my first family reconstruction
on my father's side. I am very glad because my mother's side was
the one I thought would be boring and uneventful. Two significant parts of me came out during the day: my anger, and my
dependency or inability to take care of myself.

What I have found about anger since that day is that anger is
a separating factor between two people and that it is good to be
separated for a while so as to move out in a different direction.
Even in reflecting on this event, the family reconstruction, I can
sense the anger from within. My mother never dealt with her
anger forwardly and yet she was very much in control of situations by setting up a martyr image, a "poor me" attitude, and by
putting up with so much junk from her father and my father,
which was not so good for either or all of us. My mother would
pray her way through something rather than deal with it and
move to a different place. I have seen these parts in me since then
because in experiencing anger there is change.

One powerful image of the family reconstruction was setting
up my family, sculpting them, and using a candle to symbolize
the church in the sculpt. My reaction to the candle amazes me
even now in remembering. I wanted the candle, the church, out
of the center of the sculpt and just to the front of it as a support,
not to the center. Yet the church had always been important to
me!

The importance to me? During this year as a churchgoer I have
felt great frustration with the immobility of the church, as a wom-

an in it and as one who believes in the empowerment of people. I never felt this strong a sense of it—being angry, frustrated—and feeling the same with my family—anger and frustration. These feelings in themselves are not enjoyable, but since my second family reconstruction the feelings are traveling all around and centering into myself. Also, the changes are for me. The anger is for me to use constructively, to make my own; the fear is for me to deal with and face. The places I am involved with, the people I have been close to, are changing.

At this time I'm not seriously involved with anyone. I have made no lifetime commitments, and I am free to change and create.

The family reconstructions, both of them, have given me, in effect, a new life. Don't get me wrong, this is not with rainbows, sunshine and flowers. This new life is with pain and honesty, truth and change. To enter into a family reconstruction is, if a person chooses, to change one's life, see another view, a new perspective.

So ends the story of four Explorers who reconstructed their families. Again the question: How does family reconstruction bring about these changes? The dynamics of some of these accounts are so simple. Once understood, why not the obvious change? Chris knew he wanted to be closer and more assertive with women. What kept him from doing what was so clear to him? After his family reconstruction he found himself being more assertive. What is the secret?

The following chapters will shed some light on a perennial and never fully answered question: What explains people changing?

2 WHY THIS LONG DAY'S JOURNEY?

A METAPHOR

Once upon a time there were two wolf families who lived next door to each other: one, Mr. and Mrs. Wolfgang; the other, Mr. and Mrs. Wolfonce. Each couple gave birth to a little wolf baby. Mr. and Mrs. Wolfgang named their baby Sam Wolfgang after Mr. Wolfgang's father, Grandpa Sam. Mr. and Mrs. Wolfonce named their baby Unica Wolfonce after Mrs. Wolfonce's sister, Monica.

In the Wolfgang house, little Sam was often misunderstood as he cried out for his baby needs. At other times, he was just plain neglected. As Sam grew older, he was trained to be a very good little boy. When he made mistakes, he was quickly and somewhat severely corrected so he learned that he was never to make a mistake. As Granddaddy Sam was a renowned wolf scientist, so little Sam was expected to follow in his steps. Sam was taught to stand up for his rights so that when other wolves played roughly with him he was to fight back—and win all the time. Sam had a good example for this in his father who, by fiercely competing, had become very successful as a wolf banker. In fact, by the time Sam was eight years old, his father had either bought out or forced out all the other wolf banks in the territory. To the great disappointment of his parents, Sam turned out to be a very mean wolf with all the same qualities of all mean wolves.

Mr. and Mrs. Wolfonce raised Unica by spending a great

deal of time studying her. They learned how she was such a different wolf. This was hardly a surprise as her Aunt Monica was so unique herself! In fact, the story goes that when the Wolf God made Monica, he threw the mold away! When Unica made her share of mistakes, she was corrected in such a way that she learned that mistakes are ways to learn and grow up, that mistakes are normal events. When Unica was snubbed at times by her wolf girlfriends, she was taught why that happened and told not to give up befriending them. Unica even learned that at times she felt like snubbing others and that all wolves sometimes have that same feeling. Unica grew up to be quite a unique lady wolf, and to the delight of her parents the story went about that when the Wolf God made Unica, he threw the mold away.

* * *

In order to understand family reconstruction, one must appreciate the tremendous impact the family has upon a person's development. A baby comes into the world the most dependent of all mammals. Just as it is dependent upon parents, or substitute parents, for its physical survival, it is equally dependent upon them for its emotional and mental well-being. Thus parents inevitably wield tremendous power over their children. Today it is hard for parents, who at times may feel they have no control over their children, to realize this awesome power. As children of our parents, how many of us—even at the age of 50—revert to childhood or teenage feelings and behavior when in the presence of our parents? How many of us think of ourselves as physically smaller than we are, compared to our parents? How many husbands or wives notice their spouses changing their ways of talking or behaving in the presence of their parents? All this typifies the power of the family system upon any child, even after the child becomes an adult.

Within the family system—be it natural, adoptive, blended, institutional, nuclear or extended—a person learns who, what and why he or she is. From the family of origin a person learns what to express and what to hold back, as well as how to express and how to hold back; how to respond to the entire gambit of human emotions and feelings; how to respond to various life experiences such as rejection, praise, death, birth, comings and goings, competition and cooperation, sexual stimulation, success and failure, exciting times as well as boring times. From the family we learn a set of meanings: the meaning attached to not being remembered on one's birthday and the meaning of Christmas; the meaning of being asked for a dance and of not being on time for an appointment. Most important, we learn what it means to love and be loved. These meanings are different for each person and they are indeed learned.

From the family we get our first and most impressionable understandings about how to parent, how to lead and follow, how to discipline oneself, how to delay or not delay gratification, how to deal with power, how to risk, and how to work and play. Most of our learning comes from the example of our parents. Among all these learnings there are five basic ones that permeate all that we do.

COMMUNICATION

First and foremost is the complex phenomenon of connecting with other human beings, frequently called communication, though the term connotes too limited an idea. All the ways—consciously and unconsciously, verbally and nonverbally—that we relate to others, living and dead, involve communication, a learned process built upon our innate capacities. Inadequate communication keeps intimacy from growing between two people, in spite of all their good intentions. The issue is not bad will, but incomplete modeling, principally from our family of origin.

Andrea's problems with her mother are a good example of what can happen when communication is blocked. As her mother became sharply critical of her, Andrea learned to clam up and stifle her hurt, her anger, and the bad feelings about herself she had inside. She learned to achieve intimacy with her mother by trying harder to please, even though this seemed to fail too. As she grew up, she never learned to say, "Mother, do you know how that hurts me? How that makes me feel? I feel hurt that I can never seem to please you. I feel unworthy to be your daughter. I feel like a failure. I feel so helpless."

And Andrea did not learn to go to the other power figure, her father, and explain to him what was going on inside. Nor did she learn to express her anger at her father for his not standing up to his wife when she put her down. As helpless and small children, we sense the injustice of such behavior, but we may never learn how to share thoughts and feelings in a direct, congruent way. Most of us learn to stifle or express our feelings in some skewed way, such as acting out, getting sick, or being sarcastic.

If Andrea had received some modeling on how to express her feelings straightforwardly, even if it had had no effect on her mother, Andrea's self-image and self-esteem would have been stronger. At least on her side, her communication or efforts at intimacy would have been intact, and that in itself produces self-esteem.

RULES OF BEHAVIOR

Intimately connected to communication are the rules we learn about how to behave. These rules govern us from within. They dictate every aspect of life: what feelings to show and not show ("don't be angry," "don't be afraid"), how to apply one's energy ("always do your very best"). Again, we learn these rules by watching our parents rather than by hearing them articulated. By never seeing mother and father affectionate with each other, we can learn not to be affectionate with a spouse.

Chris was constrained by one of the rules he picked up from the family in which he grew up: "Never hurt anyone." This, combined with what he learned from his father about being shy, kept Chris from being assertive with women. If you assert yourself, sometimes you will cause some hurt in another. "Never hurt anyone" is an example of a rule that inhibits human growth; it is literally impossible to go through life without hurting people. Since this is an impossible rule to keep, it is irrational—crazy if you will. Trying to follow this rule can drive a person into depression.

"Never hurt anyone" is a dehumanizing rule because it contains the universals "never" and "anyone," and these make it impossible to keep. If Chris had learned, "Avoid needlessly hurting others," then he would have been able to assert himself with Irene and Gladys, even at the risk of hurting them at times. If this had been his rule, he would not have seen himself as a failure when some of his actions inevitably hurt others. He would have integrated this into his personality and, on the deepest unconscious level, would have known that enduring hurt is as normal as eating and sleeping.

Chris learned his impossible rule—"Never hurt anyone" —unconsciously by watching his father again and again suppress his own feelings out of fear of hurting his wife, Chris's mother. On the unconscious level, something goes on like this: "This god-like person, Father, is loath to risk hurting this other divine person, Mother, so there must be something terrifying in doing that! Something terrible will happen to Mother or Father if this happens. They never cry or seem hurt. They are always strong, therefore hurt must never be! It is not to be in the human realm of things. *I must never hurt anyone.*"

Just as communication is inevitable, rules are inevitable.

There is no way we can grow up without inheriting a bundle of them. The question is: Are they irrational or rational rules? Do they free us to be truly ourselves or do they tyrannize us? Do I want to transform the rule or not?

MEANING OF BEHAVIOR

The set of meanings that we apply to any of life's experiences is learned by and large from our family of origin. One person can learn that to be late means not to love, while another person can learn that being late has little or nothing to do with loving a person. The most profound meanings of life are learned early in the home: What am I here for? What is death all about? What is suffering for? What makes for happiness? Peggy Lee's song "Is This All There Is?" is one expression of a set of meanings, while Judy Collins' song "Both Sides Now" expresses a different set of meanings. As with communication and rules, our uniquely learned set of meanings affects all we do.

For example, Chris learned what it means to be a man and a husband from observing his father: Work hard, be successful, and more than adequately support the family financially. Give in to the wife on the domestic front, making her happy by satisfying her material needs and desires. Be distant emotionally; be strong and stoical. A good husband is always strong, never weak and fearful. Chris also learned what it means to be a good wife from his mother.

What may happen is that Chris may wish to share some weakness with his female lover or wife, but stops himself because that is not what a good husband should do; he would not be fulfilling what it means to be a man and a husband. To the degree that learned meanings contravene some of Chris's natural feelings and needs, Chris will experience inner conflict.

The hope is that when Chris feels these inner conflicts, he will adjust his meanings to be congruent with his inner organism and wisdom. This is what happened to millions of Catholics who were told that using artificial birth control or masturbating was a mortal sin—sending a person to hell if unrepented. This meaning was in conflict with what they were feeling and thinking. So millions adjusted their meaning connected with birth control and masturbation. The conflict began to vanish.

It is important to note that not every inner conflict reflects a natural human need conflicting with an inappropriate meaning. Inner conflicts can spring from other sources, such as a spoiled self-centeredness conflicting with a meaning that it is good to be generous with others. The task is to take an honest look at the conflict and then decide whether or not the meaning is appropriate. Unfortunately, this may not be so easily done, as we find the prospect of changing a learned meaning too threatening.

DEALING WITH THREAT

Being threatened physically, emotionally and psychologically is such a common, inescapable reality in life that every human being learns how to deal with these threats. Since being threatened has such dire consequences, how we learn to cope with it in our families of origin is basic to survival. We can learn to deal with threats in a way that severely limits our life, or we can learn to cope with threats in a way that brings us to greater maturity. In fact, dealing with the threatening, stressful situations in life is the activity that most often spells out whether we progress or regress in our human development.

Threats can come to us from sources as varied as intimate personal relationships and international crises. The mere presence of the nuclear war threat is having a tremendous impact upon children today, as psychologists and counselors all across the United States are beginning to discover. John Mack, M.D., and others have concluded that over 50% of children of all backgrounds in the U.S. believe there will be a nuclear war before they are adults and that they will not survive. Although clinical research is not complete, Mack speculates that this may be causing children to be depressed, to distrust adult authority, and to experience difficulty in planning for the future. Various programs and methods are being tried to deal with the impact of the nuclear presence upon youngsters.[1]

Students of human behavior have identified some of the classical ways we learn to deal with threats. Karen Horney[2] says we can fight against, flee from, or go along with what is threatening us. So some protest and take action for world disarmament, some deny the existence of nuclear proliferation, while others go along with it hoping deterrence will work. A wife being abused by her husband can fight back, run out of the room, or submit to the abuse.

Virginia Satir[3] identifies five ways to cope with stress: We can blame others (therefore it's not our fault and that seems to ease us from the threat); we can placate (and get the person off our back); we can become super-reasonable (and avoid feeling anything, including the threatening feeling); we can distract ourselves and others (thus throwing the threat off course or distracting ourselves from its presence); or we can be congruent by admitting and taking responsibility for our role in the threatening scene. The first four are dysfunctional to some degree—and yet in some way they are useful. The fifth way is functional as well as useful. With credit to Virginia Satir, I use her diagrams to further illustrate these points.

[1]See, for example, Beardslee, W., and Mack, J. "The Impact of Nuclear Developments on Children and Adolescence," in *Psychosocial Aspects of Nuclear Development*, Task Force Report 20, American Psychiatric Association, Washington, DC, 1982. A work that deals with helping children is *Talking to Children About Nuclear War* by Mary Van Ornum and William Van Ornum, New York: Continuum, 1984.

[2]Horney, Karen. *Our Inner Conflicts, A Constructive Theory of Neurosis*, New York: Norton 1945, pp. 48–96.

[3]Satir, Virginia, "Patterns of Communication," Chapter 5 in *Peoplemaking*, Palo Alto, CA: Science and Behavior Books, 1972.

Figure 1. All life is basically contained in three realities: self, others, and the context of our living.

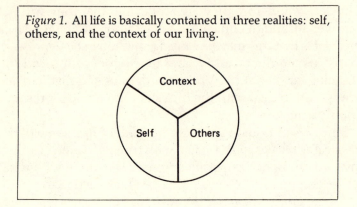

Figure 2. Blamer
   Blames others and the world: "If it weren't for you and the lousy conditions, I'd be happy."
   Defends against threat by eliminating the threat.

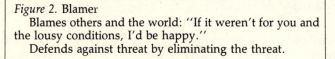
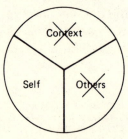

   Extreme behavior: Murder and war.
   Feeling state: Anger, power, rapid breathing, and later guilt and loneliness.
   Result: Keeps self intact, and puts others and context down. Self counts; others do not.

Figure 3. Placator
Takes blame and responsibility for all: "If it weren't for me, you'd be happy." "I do all I can to make you happy."
Defends against threat by letting the other win. Arouses guilt feelings in others so that they back off.

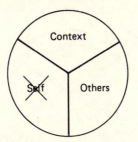

Extreme behavior: Suicide.
Feeling state: Depression, low energy, frustration, resentment, episodic rage.
Result: Maintains others to detriment of self. Others count; self doesn't.

Figure 4. Super-reasonable
Stays in the head, denying and repressing feelings: "Let's be reasonable about this and not emotional!" "Let's have the facts, ma'am."
Defends against threat by denying feelings that are the locus of experiencing threat.

Extreme behavior: Obsessive arrogance; illnesses like ulcers.
Feeling state: Little except that of being superior.
Result: Maintains ideology at expense of emotions. Ideas and the context count; feelings don't.

Figure 5. Distractor
   Does anything that is out of touch with the reality of one's thoughts, feelings and the context: "What, what's that . . . ?" "I think that . . . . Well, anyway, ... Now, where are we?"
   Defends against threat by throwing it off target or by distracting from what is threatening.

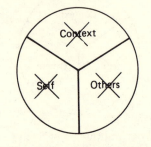

   Extreme behavior: Psychosis, alcoholism.
   Feeling state: High energy, nervousness, euphoria, fun, disconnected, out of control, inner exhaustion.
   Result: Chaos, being out of it; nothing real counts except escape.

In each of the first four types—the blamer, the placator, the super-reasonable, and the distractor—some element of reality is discounted, which makes these means of dealing with threat dysfunctional, though they do serve survival in some skewed way. The congruent method does not deny any reality; therefore it has the best chance of arriving at a solution that is real and beneficial to all. Given the inherent limitation of our creatureliness, it may not work in the sense of maintaining physical life or survival, but one's higher life—integrity, virtue, peace, self-esteem—is maintained, and the extinction of others is never risked. The congruent method is nonviolent, risky and the only way that has any chance of eliminating threat itself!

When acting congruently one's faculties correspond to what is there, what is going on. It is being on the side of objectivity rather than on the side of subjectivity. A person

Figure 6. Congruent

Takes all reality into consideration: "Let me tell you what I'm thinking and feeling, and I want to know what's going on with you. Let's stay in touch with the situation we're in."

Defends against threat by dealing with all the factors, especially the feelings, in the effort to achieve benefits for all. Tends to remove the existence of threat itself.

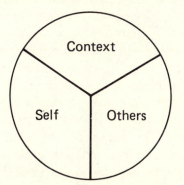

Extreme behavior: Risks death in the service of all life—the acclaimed heroes of the world (Jesus, Gandhi, Martin Luther King).

Feeling state: Trepidation at times, courage, strength and later peacefulness.

Result: All reality counts, recognizing a higher spiritual realm. It is living out the paradox of ancient wisdom: "He who loses his life, gains it."

is *aware* of what he or she is thinking, feeling, judging, deciding, wanting, and doing, and is aware of what others are also thinking, feeling, judging, deciding, wanting and doing, as well as aware of the context in which all of this is taking place. There is no denial, putting down, repressing, distorting or eliminating any of this reality. Rather, there is an attempt to deal with all of it so that the life processes of all are honored and respected in the service of human growth into peace and joy. This way of behaving is the norm for most people most of the time.

However, one of the things that can hinder acting congruently is when a person feels threatened in some way. The primal rule of self-preservation takes over. So if I need to survive by eliminating you, I'll do it. My own biological life is more important to me than anything else. This explains the phenomenon of war—self-defense (I get you before you get me). This is a primal instinctive reaction put in us to preserve our life and species. As children we operate on this instinctively, using patterns we learn from our models.

As we mature we come to recognize that in the human scheme of things there is more to life than biological preservation. Higher values and realities exist. So it has come to pass that humans are honored, called heroes and saints when they lay down their lives for their friends, relatives or even enemies! They are said to act "courageously," i.e., they overcome feeling threatened in some way so that mankind is more greatly benefitted with creative solutions by their taking into full account all of reality. This takes enormous maturity, discipline, self-control, practice, wisdom, and perhaps faith, hope and love in the sense that G. K. Chesterson speaks of it. He is reputed to have written, "Loving means to love that which is unlovable, forgiving means to pardon the unpardonable, faith means believing the unbelievable, hope means hoping when things are hopeless or it is no virtue at all." This type of thinking and behaving assumes a deeper understanding of life and reality than meets the eye.

Fortunately most threats are not serious enough and longlasting enough that the congruent behavior of the Gandhi type is called for. One of the signs of human growth is how frequently I find myself dealing with threat in a congruent way rather than in a blaming, placating, distracting or superreasonable way.

It is not always easy to judge whether one is acting congruently or not. A common mistake is to be so reasonable that one ignores any anger and resentment that may be present. People tend to suppress or pretend that anger is not within them in the service of being congruent. Anger should be harnessed and used productively. Those who pretend that anger is not present when it is are certainly not being congruent.

In *Cat on a Hot Tin Roof*,[4] we see examples of all these defense methods. Big Daddy, the head of the family, is a blamer. Big Mama, the dutiful wife, is a placator. Brick, the favorite son, is a distractor, especially by his drinking. Maggie, starved for Brick's affection and financially insecure, moves from blaming to placating. While basically a placator, Gooper, the obedient, responsible son, periodically relies on super-reasonableness. The one moment of congruence comes with Brick's confrontation of Big Daddy over his fatal illness, bringing a spark of hope that there may be some escape from their dehumanizing and unreal pattern of living. The tragedy is that it looks as though it won't happen.

I invite the reader to reread the first chapter of this book and identify the five ways of dealing with threat. One way of viewing the goal of family reconstruction is to see it as an effort to get the Explorer to act in a congruent way during the day. When this happens, the day is a journey into light!

THE BASIC RULE OF SURVIVAL

Somewhere down deep each of us has learned that of all the things that can threaten us there is one thing that threatens us more than any other. It is the one thing above all that distresses us the most when triggered. Virginia Satir calls this the *basic rule of survival*. I can't think of a better label for it. When that part of us is threatened, all of our buttons are pushed. It is as if we learned, "If so-and-so happens to me, I'll die or I'll be wiped out."

The threat of psychological death may be worse than con-

[4]Williams, Tennessee. *Cat on a Hot Tin Roof*. New York: Norton, 1975.

templation of physical death. Some people can more readily cope with the threat of physical death than face some other events. For example, some men would rather die on a battlefield than become sexually impotent. Some may valiantly fight fatal cancer but collapse when financially bankrupt. Others would rather die than be dominated by a mother figure. In the face of this threat to our survival, we will do anything—even to the severe detriment of ourselves or others—to avoid it. What we do to avoid or cope with this threat is learned.

The basic rule of survival is so deeply embedded that I have found it the hardest element to unearth in therapy. Often I think, "Ah, at last we have uncovered it," only to find the basic rule for survival is something else. When I began working with Chris, for example, I thought his most basic rule of survival was "Never be angry or else I won't love you" (perceived by a child, that could mean you'll die if I won't love you). However, it became clear later that the basic rule for Chris was "Never hurt anyone," stemming from his fear of hurting Irene and Gladys and from seeing his Dad never hurt them. "Never hurt anyone or else you'll die" or " . . . or else you won't matter to us" could lead Chris to behavior like suppressing his anger and failing to assert himself. This could keep him from being truly himself and from really living.

This basic rule can dominate and control our actions so profoundly that we find ourselves living unhappily, protecting this sometimes rather absurd fear. Some of these catastrophes are the making of the mind and have precious little to do with reality, especially when adulthood has been reached. That is why I consider the rule of survival to be so pervasive and list it as one of the most important learnings that we pick up from our family experience.

* * *

From our family of origin we then learn five things that affect our entire lives: how to relate to others, a set of rules to live by, a set of meanings about life experiences, a way of handling threats, and ways to deal with the greatest calamity that can befall us.

Why do these lessons coming from the modeling of our parents imprint themselves so strongly in us—so strongly that for many it is extremely difficult to change or modify these learnings? (Thank heaven many of our learnings are helpful, liberating, growth-inducing and therefore welcomed by us!) The answer lies in the fact that since children literally depend on their parents for survival, they must comply with parental wishes to survive. Thus, parents have a god-like power. What they do means life or death to the offspring—physically and psychologically. Add to this the child's constant awareness of his or her limitations—falling, spilling food and drink, wetting pants—in contrast to the parents' usually flawless behavior. This presents another god-like impression for the child: Parents are all powerful and perfect! These learnings come to the child with "divine authority." No wonder these teachings are so powerfully conveyed to a newborn child open to receiving all. Also keep in mind that these learnings are grasped not purely in the mental apparatus of the person but, more importantly, in the emotional system as well. These learnings are received and absorbed by the entire human psyche.

To dislodge these learnings so as to transform them, if desired, requires a powerful emotional new experience—a total psychological experience, not just an intellectual insight. Many times this must take place with the parents (or surrogate parents) from whom the learnings were originally received. Parenthetically, many theorists believe that when young people choose their marriage mates, they pick someone with whom they can carry on this unfinished business from mother and father. They use the new spouse to unravel the old learnings and to transform them so as to deal with life differently. Since in many cases this transformation needs to be done with mother and father in order to get to the emotional level required for such dislodgement, we find the usefulness of family reconstruction.

In a family reconstruction, instead of having the real parents involved, the parents and other family members are played by other group members. Role players can in most cases create a more powerful situation than the real family; many times it is safer and easier for the Explorer to express feelings more accurately and strongly with role players than with members of the family. The dislodgement of old embedded learnings can get a forceful beginning during a family reconstruction.

The actual family reconstruction is usually an all-day affair. The Explorer prepares for the day by doing some homework, which takes from five to 20 hours, depending on how extensive the Explorer wants to be. (This work will be explained later in the book.) On the day itself, 12 to 30 people gather, and the Explorer chooses from among the persons who will assume roles of various members of his immediate family of origin and members of his mother's and father's family. Then certain scenes of these families' home lives are reconstructed and reenacted. It is amazing how well the role players can get into their parts and play out the scenes. Some of the recurring remarks heard from Explorers include statements like: "How accurate this all is!" "My mother said what you just said!" "Have you been in my home?" "Do you know my father?"

These scenes become so alive that they stir up deep and powerful emotional reactions in the Explorer; it is almost as if these scenes were actually occurring again. The Guide invites the Explorer to enter into a scene when something is awakened within. This allows the Explorer to have new and different experiences with mother, father, grandparents, aunts and uncles, brothers and sisters. To the degree that the new experience is emotionally intense, the Explorer gains new learnings from the scene that differ from what he or she may have learned in the original family experience. Thus, the original communication patterns, rules, meanings, coping mechanisms and rule of survival are being dislodged. The pathway to transformation is opened. Many of the patterns that the Explorer learned from his family are no longer serviceable to him in his adult life, so he begins to learn new ways of handling himself and situations.

For example, the Explorer may have learned not to show affection readily. This may be a problem now within his marriage, so he would like to break that pattern and learn to be more affectionate. Or the Explorer may have learned to do all in life to make her husband happy. Now she wishes to learn how to assert her own needs as well.

Recently a couple came to me in great distress. She was devastated by the bomb he had dropped three days earlier: "I'm separating from you for a while—I need to straighten some things out—I've met someone else." She couldn't understand why his love for her had died: "I love you so much. I've done all I could over the years to make you happy. If you wanted to hike, I did, even though I didn't enjoy it. Anything you wanted to do I did, even when I didn't really want to . . . " But on the hike she complained a lot. Now that is to be expected when one is doing something one really doesn't want to do. When a person is always putting her own wants on the back burner, a general dissatisfaction with life emerges and gets expressed through complaining.

After years of what he perceived as negativism and after years of what she perceived as sacrificing to make him happy out of love, he lost his feelings for her and she couldn't understand why her love was spurned! Now she wants to change this pattern. She wants to feel some satisfaction in life from getting some of her own needs met by him instead of only giving in to his needs. If he is open to try this more functional way of behaving, there is some hope for the relationship.

Other dysfunctional patterns commonly learned in families include the fear of closeness with another person, the pretense of having no feelings, the need to boost one's self-esteem by being better than others, and the desire to get one's own way all the time. In a family reconstruction the Guide invites the Explorer to operate differently in some of the original scenes where he learned dysfunctional patterns. When this happens—and especially when it takes great effort—the Explorer gets unstuck and is already on the road to using new learnings in his life. After the reconstruction, the Explorer gradually moves into these new ways of feeling, perceiving and behaving, so that with time he can surely transform a blaming pattern to a responsible one or an inhibiting pattern to one of expressing affection.

In addition to dislodging a dysfunctional pattern, the family reconstruction can bring other results. The Explorer sees things in a reenacted scene never seen before, which leads toward a new and more mature understanding. For example, a young boy who hears his father threaten to leave in the heat of an argument may fear that "if you argue you will lose your loved one." Therefore, the child unconsciously decides never to argue. The Explorer can use his maturity to see—and intensely *experience*—that Dad didn't really mean that! He can learn that arguments won't necessarily lead to desertion—a tremendously important new meaning. This seems almost absurd. Surely any person can see that arguments don't evitably lead to abandonment. Yet when such ideas are imprinted early in life, pure common sense has little impact on actually overcoming them.

During the family reconstruction the Explorer can get in touch with aspects of mother and father that were hidden from him as a child, things like their sexuality, their early romantic dreams, their inner fears, their longings for love and affection, their disappointments, their awkward ways as newlyweds, their guilt, their excitement with their babies, their sadness in losing their parents. The Explorer now perceives his mother and father as normal human beings rather than as gods. As a result of seeing his parents as humans making their share of mistakes, the Explorer can more easily transform learnings bestowed by parents; he can realize that these learnings now come from humans rather than from "God." It helps the Explorer to *experience*, not just *know*, that what he is trying to do in his life is exactly what mother and father were trying to do in their lives. The Explorer sees how his parents learned from their families and how the newlyweds combined these patterns in building the family the Explorer came from. The Explorer also sees how Mom and Dad had the same contentions with their parents that the Explorer has. The Explorer sees that his parents were struggling to get for themselves love, respect, understanding and happiness, and that perhaps they were fighting for them in precisely the same way the Explorer is now. All this allows the Explorer to have a compassionate understanding of his parents as human beings.

Dynamically what is at stake is this: The child is unable, due to his immaturity, to see and understand all that is taking place before him. The child also has a black-and-white view of the world; people are seen as either good guys or bad guys. A child's mind can't grasp the grays and subtleties of human life. So the construction of the family experience put together by a child is far from whole and accurate. Often it is full of distortions and deletions. Sometimes, based on these inaccurate perceptions, a child can form emotional responses and make serious lifelong decisions and judgments about himself regarding what value he holds and how he should live. Also, the child, basically in a receiving state, is vulnerable and dependent on what is being given to him. Thus the early lessons are deeply embedded. The family reconstruction process allows the adult—who now has the capacity to see more, understand more completely, and appreciate the complexities of the human situation—to get a new construction of the family experience. With the new perceptions and consequent feelings, the adult is in a better position to make decisions and changes in his life.

It is critical that the new view be followed by a new set of feelings for an integrated transformation to occur. This does not involve radical cutting out or total rebuilding; rather, the Explorer adds to or modifies earlier perceptions. And all this happens in a powerful way because the family reconstruction gives a person the best chance to do all this with strong emotional affect.

Does each family reconstruction have these marvelous results? No. Much depends on the Explorer's commitment to change. Has the Explorer arrived at the proper moment in life or not? Is he truly fed up and ready for a new way— strange and scary as that new way may be? Other important factors are the trust the Explorer has in the Guide and in the group; the amount of loving energy present in the group and in the Guide; and the skill, knowledge, experience, intuition, creativity and caring of the Guide. If all these are present, then it is off to the moon. The long day will indeed end in light!

The results can be immediate, but most often the solid results are long in coming. The family reconstruction is a beginning; it's a powerful new birth. The results of the family reconstruction can be physically felt, as well as woven into new patterns of life. The usual physical reaction is one of being drained in a cleansing sense: body limp and relaxed, with a sense of emotional peace. A feeling of thorough exhaustion may set in. Some people may become quite stirred up and confused. Others may feel some physical sickness. What surprises me is the drained feeling expressed by those whose family reconstructions didn't appear to be very emotional. What appeared to me to be a small amount of emotion was really a big amount for them! For some the results are less dramatic and powerful. Family reconstruction may be just a moderate reentry into the past, resulting in a few new insights and appreciations, and some gradual changes.

Family reconstruction can also powerfully influence the members of the group, whether they play a role or not. Group members can easily get caught up in what they are seeing or acting out. Their emotions rise; they identify themselves and their families with the personal and familial systems unfolding before their eyes. The result is that for some members of the group a cartharsis is effected—sometimes more powerful than that of the Explorer.

Even those in the group who withdraw from involvement because of feeling threatened in some way can learn that something is going on that is pushing them. Perhaps later on, in a more nonthreatening environment, they can look back on the experience and see what threatened them and learn more deeply about themselves.

One of the powerful experiences of a Family Reconstruction is the dynamics of the group itself. The Guide is open and caring; there is an absence of put-downs; freedom to express oneself is encouraged; sharing of honest feelings takes place; people can ask for what they want, can express what bothers them and what they appreciate. This open system can be a refreshingly new experience for many not accustomed to such growth-producing processes. In effect, the members spend a day functioning in an open system, dealing with some of the most basic issues of life. Change in our lives may come from having a powerful human experience that runs counter to a dysfunctional experience.

When a family reconstruction is finished, the Guide should have a session or two with the Explorer (or the Explorer can utilize his own therapist or counselor), since the process will most likely stir up deep feelings, different perceptions and a new self-image in the Explorer. These stirrings will continue for many weeks and months.

Sometimes you will hear of a "complete" family reconstruction, as opposed to a "partial" or "mini" family reconstruction. A complete family reconstruction fully explores both the maternal and paternal family systems to discover the learnings the Explorer's mother and father brought into their marriage. Also included is an exploration of the family of origin so the Explorer can see how those learnings brought by the parents combined in their marriage in such a way that the Explorer learned his or her coping mechanisms, survival rules, etc. All this exploration is done in a life-like manner, so as to engage the Explorer in a *total* psychological experience. As a result, the Explorer *relates differently* to mother, father and other family members during the reconstruction. Therefore, the Explorer not only sees new things (content) but has the new experience of communicating congruently, using transformed functional rules, and of coping in straight ways (process). This results in humanizing the parents and raising the Explorer's self-worth.

Anything short of this is a partial or mini reconstruction. Examples of partial reconstructions are: exploring only one of the three families; isolating only one scene that reveals only one dysfunctional rule or coping mechanism; dealing with only one incongruous communication pattern; doing a piece of work so that insight is the result rather than a total psychological experience; helping a person deal with a problem without unlocking and transforming the pattern beneath the problem. These partial reconstructions can be powerful and extremely valuable, but they are not full family reconstructions.

It is also important to realize that there is no one way to bring about a full family reconstruction. One may be done mainly by sculpting, another by more verbal descriptions of family members and scenes, another by using pantomime as well as psychodrama. Each reconstruction will contain different scenes, though some basic classical ones are usually reconstructed: mother and father growing up, the courtship and marriage of the Explorer's parents, an elaborate birthing of the Explorer, the births of siblings, deaths of siblings and parents. One reconstruction may take three hours while another may take three days.

With this brief overview of the whys and wherefors of family reconstruction, we are now ready to go on to the step-by-step explanation and description of how it is done and what takes place during the day.

3 THE EXPLORER GATHERS THE SUPPLIES

The Explorer must prepare carefully for the day's journey into reconstructing the family. He researches and gathers a host of facts about his family. The length of time this takes depends upon the zeal of the Explorer and the accessibility of the data.

This preparation consists of four parts: the circle of influence, the family trees, the chronology, and the birth fantasies. I suggest that the circle of influence be done first since this is the easiest and stimulates the memory for the rest of the work. Then the family trees, the chronology, and the birth fantasies should be done in that order. I give out the instruction sheets that follow to aid the Explorer in his preparation. I strongly urge you to do this work for your own benefit as well as to get a sense of how this preparation generates feelings and insights in the Explorer.

My clients are greatly helped by doing this work even if they do not go through an actual family reconstruction. As one man said to me, "I never realized how my life's pattern is so much like my father's." Another said, "I felt sad at the end. I have so much unfinished business with my parents. I feel an emptiness. I must get on with this task."

This homework intensifies the motivation to get on with one's therapy. As the chapters of the book unfold, you will see how information and insights raised by this preparation will be used to help clients through the fantasy and sculpting processes both in family reconstructions and in private sessions.

The Circle of Influence

Put your name in a circle in the center of a piece of paper and draw spokes out from it for each person who had something to do with your rearing from birth to 18 years. Be sure to list those who had a negative as well as positive influence. Put the names of those who had greater influence at the end of shorter, thicker spokes and those of lesser influence at the end of longer, thinner spokes. For each person, write the name, the role the person played, and an adjective or brief phase describing how you experienced their influence. When you finish the task, write down your feelings. The following is a sample:

Figure 7. Circle of influence

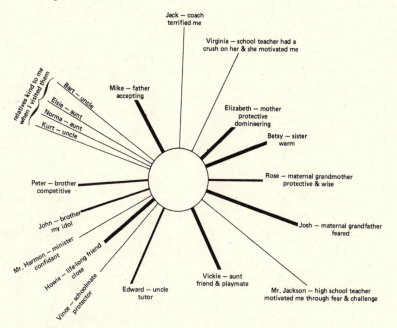

Feelings: How fortunate I was to have good people around me during my early years. A sense of gratitude and being blessed.

Family Trees

Draw three family trees or genograms as exemplified by the following pages. The first one is the family of your origin, the other two are the families of your mother and father. Dates of births, deaths, marriages, divorces are listed. If the date is not available, make an educated guess and put a question mark beside the date. List a couple of adjectives that describe the personalities as you perceived them. Also describe the way mother and father, parent and child related to each other as exemplified by the sample. Include any significant others who may have lived in the home, such as grandparents, cooks, nannies, etc. Write down your feelings at the end of doing this.

Figure 8. Symbols to describe family members and structure

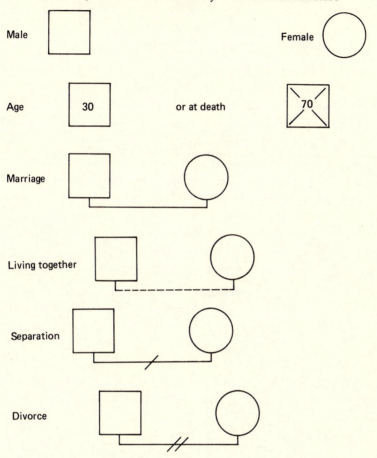

Male

Female

Age   30   or at death   70

Marriage

Living together

Separation

Divorce

Children — list in birth order beginning with oldest on left

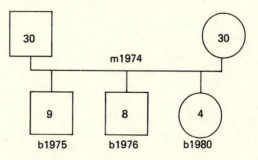

30   m1974   30

9   8   4
b1975   b1976   b1980

Family Reconstruction

Figure 8 (continued).

Adopted or foster children

Fraternal twins

Identical twins

Spontaneous abortion

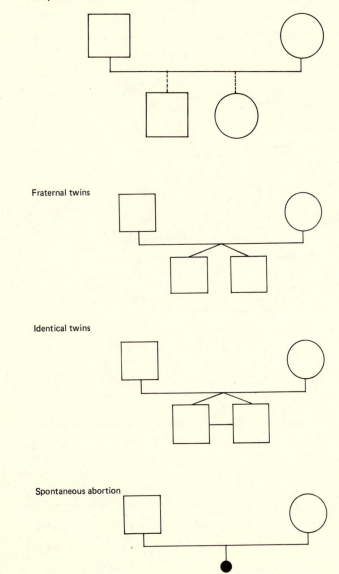

Figure 8 (continued).

Induced abortion

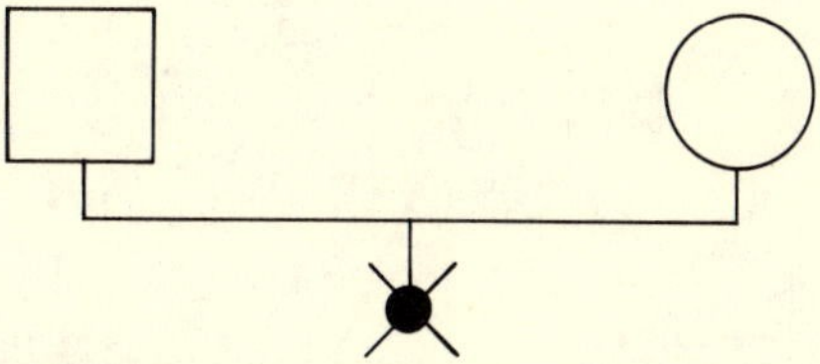

Stillborn

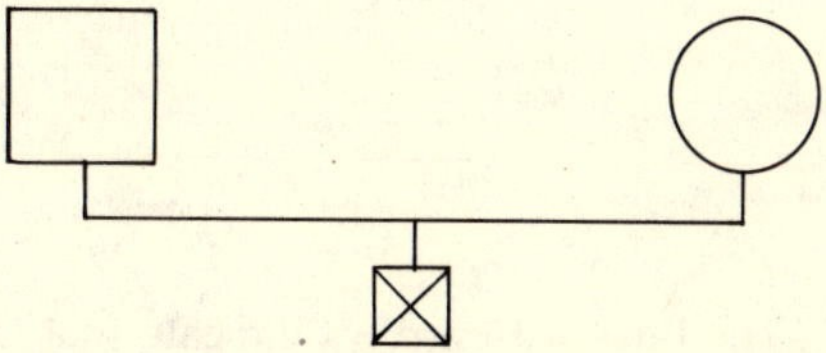

Figure 9. Daniel Bacon's *family of origin* (recorded 1984)

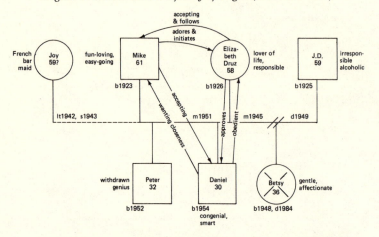

The lines with arrows indicate that Daniel sees that he related to his father by wanting more closeness and that Mike accepted Daniel. Elizabeth accepted and followed her husband Mike, while he adored and took a leadership role with his wife, Elizabeth. This family tree represents the way Daniel perceived these people and the important relationships between his parents and himself.

Figure 10. Daniel Bacon's *father's family* (recorded 1984)

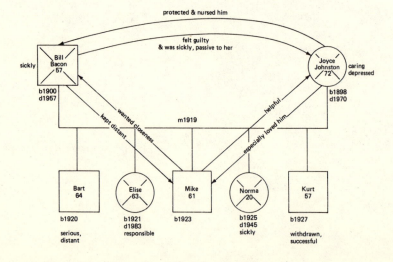

Figure 11. Daniel Bacon's *mother's family* (recorded 1984)

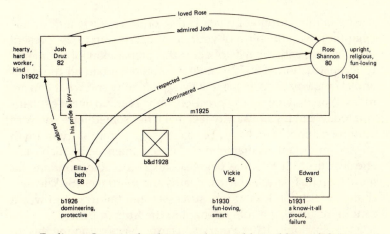

Feelings: Surprised at how mother and her siblings didn't turn out better, given their parents. Sad at how great things could have been with some slight changes in family history.

Family Chronology

The family chronology is a listing of dates, facts and events beginning with the birth of your grandparents up to the present time, ending with the date of doing this preparation for your family reconstruction. This chronology should contain all the dates and events you think in some way explain who and what you are today. You may not know precisely how a certain event explains you today, but if you vaguely feel that it has something to do with your formation, then list it. For example, a family story or myth may be important, as many times we are influenced by such a tale and live up to it to some degree. This chronology contains far more than just dates of births, deaths and marriages. Sicknesses, change of school, loss of job, successes and failures, and world conditions all play a role in shaping the human being.

Many Explorers have a marvelous experience gathering this information from their parents and other living relatives. Often it draws them closer together. Parents and relatives are flattered when asked about their lives.

Divide the chronology into three sections: the paternal family, the maternal family, and the family of origin. The family of origin begins with that date and event in which father and mother met each other in a dating way for the first time. When you guess a date or event, put a question mark next to it. When you're finished, write down your feelings.

SAMPLE CHRONOLOGY OF GUS O'MEARA

Paternal

1858	Joseph O'Meara born in N. Ireland
1860	Mary Hanrahan born in S. Ireland
1879 (?)	Joseph & Mary meet in U.S. after immigrating from Ireland
1880	Joseph and Mary marry in Topeka, Kansas
1882	Marie O'Meara, first child of Joseph & Mary, is born
1883	O'Meara family moves to Kansas City, and Joseph opens a saloon

1884   John O'Meara (my father) is born
1886   A stillbirth
1888   Martha is born
1894   Marie is killed in fall from climbing a tree
1904   Joseph dies, and John begins to support the family
1909 (?) Mary gets mysteriously ill and is confined to a
         wheelchair
• other dates   [There can be as many as 30 to 50 entries,
• and events   depending on how much is known about the
• until   family.]
1922   John meets Jane (my mother) at a friend's house

Maternal

1861   Edward Johansen born in Sweden
1863   Gertrude Nelson born in Norway
1883   Edward meets Gertrude in New York City at work
• other dates
• and events
• until
1922   Jane meets John (my father) at a friend's house

Family of origin

[Usually there are more entries here than in the paternal and
maternal families since more is known about one's family of
origin.]

1924   John & Jane get engaged in Topeka, Kansas
1925   John & Jane married in Kansas City, Missouri, by a
         Justice of the Peace
1929   Gus (me) is born
1929   John is promoted by Hallmark and they move to
         San Francisco
1930   Janice is born premature
1932   Miscarriage
1933   a stillbirth
1934   Jackie is born
1936   Family buys big house on Nob Hill

1937   Gus gets straight A's on report card and is given a
          two-week trip to summer camp
1937   At summer camp, Gus meets Sam, who becomes
          his lifelong buddy
  •
  •
  •
1984   Gus is preparing for his family reconstruction

Feelings: Overwhelmed with how lucky everything turned
out for me, how fortunate I've been. I feel some sense of
obligation to do good in payment for my good fortune. I
wonder how those deaths affected mother?

Birth Fantasies

Write down your fantasy of the births of your mother, father and yourself. You may know only the dates and places of these births, so simply make up the rest of the story. Put in whatever facts you know, but do not let the absence of information inhibit the flight of your imagination.

Sample: Birth of my Mother, Marge

It was a bitter cold February 8, 1924. Jennie had told her loving husband Jack that she felt the time was close for their third child's birth. Jack informed the neighbors to watch over Jennie this day while he was at work. At 10 a.m. Jennie told Susie to call Jack at the bank to come to take her to the hospital . . . etc. to end of fantasy.

Feelings: How delightful I felt in doing this. I wonder if Mother's birth was actually this problem-free?!? I'll have to check it out with her when I see her at Christmas.

Preparation for the family reconstruction takes the Explorer into these three families, rather than into just the immediate family of origin, since the Explorer will need to see how father and mother were raised to be the kind of people they were when they married. Then the Explorer has the opportunity to see how they blended together to form their family system with its rules, coping mechanisms, sets of meanings and ways of relating. This also presents the chance to see how certain patterns may have been transmitted from generation to generation and how the Explorer may be repeating the same pattern in his or her own marriage of today. In the live reconstruction, the Explorer will see how the dysfunctional patterns could have been changed if certain things had happened, such as a member sharing feelings honestly. This often allows the Explorer to see ways of changing his own patterns.

I urge the Explorer to make a first draft of the homework to see how much information he or she already possesses. Then the Explorer can do further research to fill in the empty spaces. Many times the contact the Explorer makes with father, mother, brother, sister in getting this data is very rewarding in itself. Often the Explorer is surprised to see how Dad opens up in a way that he has never done before, or how flattered the parents are to find their son or daughter being interested in their families. Sometimes a parent of an Explorer can be very threatened by such inquiries. How the parent is threatened can reveal important rules at work, such as "Don't tell family secrets" or "Don't mention sex." How the parent is threatened (forgetting the event or being distracted, for example) can reveal how he or she copes with pain.

If the Explorer persists in a gentle nonthreatening way, a parent may open up on a subject for the first time in his or her life. This opening-up can be very healing for the parent, as well as for the Explorer. A rich closeness is achieved between parent and son or daughter. So at times the very work that needed to be done during the family reconstruction is accomplished in the very process of preparing for the day itself!

Writing the three birth fantasies is very important. The object is not to record the facts of the birth but to see how the Explorer creates the fantasy. From these fantasies I can get some clues as to how the Explorer feels about himself and about his parents.

Sometimes the fantasy will consist of only facts with little emotion. Some will be skimpy and others very detailed. There may be a significant difference in the portrayal of the parents. One may be very warm and cheerful in tone while the other is cold and abstract. One may be dutiful and the other relaxed. All this can help the Guide gather hunches before the reconstruction. For example, one Explorer, Pete, had a bare-boned birth fantasy. This was consistent with his poor self-esteem. I decided that it would be crucial for Pete to spend a great deal of time reenacting his own birth during his reconstruction. It would be important for him to experience the variety of feelings his mother had at the time, since his fantasy revealed little emotion.

Explorers are amazed by how much they get from doing these fantasies. I recall doing my own. It was a warm and nurturing experience for me to fantasize all the love and attention I got. I fantasized who was there at the birth and how excited they were. I fantasized that my favorite Aunt Jo was there. (Later Mother told me that in fact she was!) Doing this made me feel warm and good about myself and added to my self-esteem.

The birth fantasies are important because as things begin so they tend to continue in life as well as in therapy. It takes enormous energy to overcome initial mistakes. For example, if I begin a family reconstruction and do not warm up the group, build trust and help participants get connected, then the rest of the day will be spent coping with the lack of trust and the poor beginning. Many of the people I have helped through the years have had something go wrong at the time of their births—a mother who was under stress, or who harbored abnormal fears regarding the birth, poor production of milk, rejection of the mother's breast, long separation from mother due to premature birth, lack of support from father. Perhaps the parents didn't want the pregnancy, or had a tragedy befall them prior to the birth. Perhaps the parents held exaggerated expectations for the new child (for example, this baby will make our marriage work, or this baby will make up for the one who died, or this baby will make me happy in this unhappy marriage). The fantasies can reveal some of these elements.

With the circle of influence, family trees, chronology and birth fantasies in hand, the Explorer has all the supplies necessary for the day's journey.

4 IMMEDIATE PREPARATIONS FOR THE JOURNEY

PLOTTING THE ROAD

After the Explorer gathers the supplies, he or she brings the work to the Guide, who then interviews the Explorer. In the interview the Guide discovers what the Explorer wants to achieve in the reconstruction. For example, Andrea (see Chapter 1) wanted a new way of relating to her mother, while Chris wanted to become more assertive and be rid of his ulcer. Often, however, the conscious desire of the Explorer gives way to a more important but unconscious achievement as the family reconstruction ensues. One Explorer, Joan, honestly was not aware of any specific issue she wanted to deal with, yet something was urging her to do her family reconstruction. During the reconstruction the problem emerged that she seldom reaches out for what she really wants in life. She was always doing what others wanted of her. Even in the interview she didn't know how to reach out for what she wanted!

The second thing the Guide must determine is what dilemma the Explorer is currently facing. This is a critical issue that focuses scenes the Guide might set up in the reconstruction as well as what to look for as it proceeds. For example, Sam said he wanted to find out more about his father and his father's family. He also said that the dilemma he was facing in his life, and had always faced, was that he didn't know how to be forceful without putting others down. As soon as I discovered that, I had a focus and I knew what to look for in his father and his father's family. Was the father that way? If so, was Sam raised that way? How could I let Sam see his father acting differently? What kept his father from doing this? Or was it his mother who was like this and, if so, what role did the father have in it? So Sam's current dilemma gave a focus to the family reconstruction more than his answer to what he wanted to get out of it. Going into the past, just for the past's sake, is very rewarding—especially if new pictures and insights are seen. However, tying the past to the present dilemma gives relevance to the family reconstruction.

The Guide's third goal is to find out what fears the Explorer has and then to deal with those fears. Usually there is a general anxiety about going into the unfamiliar places and discovering something that may be threatening. When the anxiety is high I ask the Explorer, "What would be the worst thing you might discover about your family?" As soon as the Explorer expresses his worst fear, the apprehension tends to lessen. I confirm that something new will be discovered and that the unfamiliar will most likely be uncomfortable for a while. It is true that many people, during or after a family reconstruction, experience some anger toward a parent that they never knew was inside of them. Many Explorers fear what others in the group will think of them. I prefer to deal with that fear on the day of the reconstruction itself.

Fourth, the Guide asks what the Explorer wants from the Guide during the reconstruction. Most of what the Explorer wants from the Guide is implicit and assumed, such as love, caring, gentleness, being in control. This fourth question is good, though, as it gives permission to the Explorer to put some explicit demands on the Guide. For example, the Explorer may not want some personal information or event revealed to the group. One may want the Guide to push against her fear and resistances while another wants the Guide to go easy with him on this score.

I usually bring up the matter of resistance (if the Explorer hasn't done so) as the fifth issue of the interview. I explain that I shall push the Explorer gently beyond any resistance that appears. Should the Explorer really buck during the reconstruction, however, I will make clear what is happening and see what he or she wishes to do about it. I respect these resistances as ways people protect themselves, and I do not want to tear them down in a manipulative way. By dealing openly with them when they arise, I can be guided by the Explorer. I let the Explorer know that progress is made when we can go beyond old boundaries, and that is the reason for my gently urging when I detect resistance. However, if the area being resisted is too threatening, we can simply acknowledge that fact, and pass on. I must note that few Explorers continue to resist.

I try to remember that everything need not be achieved in a given day, that each person has a rightful moment for growth, and that what seems a small gain in my view may be a large gain for the Explorer. *Being closely in touch with and guided by the Explorer at all times is absolutely critical.* It is not mine, but the Explorer's own day, agenda (conscious or unconscious), growth, and reconstruction.

A common cause of resistance is the need that many have to hold onto an old perception or picture of a parent (for example, that mother is a saint and father a scum). The Explorer has built a life and way of feeling around those perceptions. To allow a different, usually more human, picture calls for unlocking a whole chain of feelings and behavior. This can be threatening. One's self-image is linked in some way to those old perceptions. It sounds strange to think a person would be loath to change a negative perception to a more human one, but often that is the case. An instance of this occurred when one Explorer, Mary, resisted seeing that her father had some good points and refused to understand his side of the story of why he "abandoned" the family when Mary was three years old. Her perception of her father had been formed by the anger and hatred of her mother toward him. Mary resisted the new perception of her father because if she accepted the new perception of him being portrayed in the psychodrama, then in some unconscious way she would be betraying her mother. And Mary's perception of herself was that of a fiercely loyal daughter to her mother.

Earlier I mentioned that one of the things the Explorer may want from me is not to reveal some embarrassing event in his personal life. Dealing with this becomes another goal of the interview. If the event is one that occurred later in the Explorer's life, like a prison sentence, I point out that we don't usually deal with later events. We are interested in seeing how his early years contributed to establishing the communication patterns, coping mechanisms, and sets of meanings that are influencing his life now. Our goal is to reconstruct those formative experiences.

If the event does have real impact on the person's present life—if the Explorer, for instance, is embarrassed about incest—then I show how even in that event what is most important is what the Explorer learned prior to the event that set up the reactions and ways of coping that resulted. If the Explorer coped by never speaking about it to anyone, then in some way a rule about family secrets (or about sex or about never hurting anyone) could have been learned in that family that rendered the Explorer speechless. I point out how dysfunctional that learning was and how it is still operating! In the family reconstruction it is more important to deal with that dysfunctional pattern in order to give freedom to the Explorer to operate on a more functional rule than it is to deal with the specifics of the event (the incest, for example). From that point of view, we need not mention the incest at all. However, I also point out to the Explorer that if in the course of the family reconstruction he wants to mention it, then in the very process for the second time in his life he has broken the old rule! After all this I have yet to have an Explorer want to keep a secret. If I ever do encounter one who does want it kept hidden, then I will abide by that person's wishes, realizing that growth is made in steps.

During the interview the Explorer may state a desire to invite some relatives to the family reconstruction. I have had Explorers bring spouses, parents, children, siblings. The result has always been highly rewarding. In the interview I make three points:

1) The family members must be told that each has a personal picture of the family that will differ in some ways from that of the Explorer. They are to refrain from objecting to the perceptions of the Explorer, respecting instead the reality of each person's experience of the family—if for no other reason than different birth order. *At no time does a relative play his or her own role during the reconstruction.* Seldom is it advisable to allow family members to play any other roles. Too often close relatives are too enmeshed in their own feelings and reactions to discover more deeply hidden feelings that are there and need to be brought to the surface for the benefit of the Explorer. A role player will be able to get in touch with the full set of feelings. Also, the Explorer is charged with strong feelings that will be triggered by the actual relative playing himself, which will prevent the Explorer from being aware of other internal states, such as anger and desire for closeness.

2) The Explorer must not be intimidated by the presence of the family members. If in any way the Explorer would not be completely free to be himself or herself, then the relatives should not be invited.

3) I tell the Explorer that a rich opportunity may arise to involve the relatives in some way—by asking questions of them or engaging them in conversation over some unfinished business. I ask the Explorer for permission to act upon such an opportunity if it arises. An example of this was Elfie. She

discovered during the reconstruction that she had learned as a child to deny pain and not ask for help. In a flash of insight she realized that she had been doing this during the 25 years of her marriage. Her husband was at the reconstruction. We spent the last hour of the day negotiating a contract with both of them outlining how he could respond differently to her pain and how she could ask for his help. We discussed how she could cope with her husband if he became too threatened by her requests and how there are other ways to cope rather than just shutting down. During that hour new ground was broken in a 25-year marriage!

At the end of the interview I usually sum up what we have done so far.

THE EXPLORING PARTY GETS SET

Doing a family reconstruction requires a sufficient number of people to play the roles of the different family members. Although I have had groups as small as seven and as large as 90, a group of 15 to 20 seems optimal. A group of this size is large enough to allow the Explorer a sufficient variety of people from which to pick role players closely resembling the various family members. It is small enough so that almost every person will be chosen to play a part and become actively engaged in the work of the day. This is not to imply that a person never chosen to play a role cannot be powerfully affected by watching the family reconstruction. Often an observer will get caught up in the drama or in one of the members, and then have the opportunity (by not being a role player) to withdraw internally from the action to make personal connections and applications to his own life.

There are different ways to form a group. The Explorer can simply invite friends. Some therapists invite professional colleagues and sometimes charge them a fee, as they are

learning for themselves both personally and professional-
ly. Groups are easily formed in residential treatment centers.

Former students of mine have been so convinced of the
benefits of family reconstruction that they have formed ongoing groups. I have had groups of about 12 people who
meet once a month for a year; each month a different person does a family reconstruction. Some of these groups are
made up mainly of clients whom I feel could especially gain
from doing their family reconstructions. I teach classes in
family reconstruction and at least one family reconstruction
is done in the class.

A friend of mine has put together groups by visiting Al-
Anon meetings and explaining the power and effects of
family reconstruction. Those recovering from chemical dependency such as alcoholism are vitally interested in reconstructing their families, as they see their disease as a family issue as well as a personal one.

When the members of the group gather on the day of the
family reconstruction, they are strangers to each other in one
of two ways: this may be their first meeting, or they may
not have seen one another for a month and during that
month each one has changed to some degree. While they
are united by a common purpose, they need to be bonded
in a deeper, more trusting way to undertake such an intimate journey as a person's family reconstruction. One of
the critical dynamics making for an effective reconstruction
is the loving energy for the Explorer within the group. For
this energy to be developed and released, trust and warmth
and a family way of thinking need to be fostered in the participants. This loving energy is an invisible force that oper-
ates through the day. Other contributing factors are: the
commitment or motivation of the Explorer; the bonding between the Explorer and the Guide; the skillful resources of
the Guide; and the arrival of the Explorer at "that time in
one's life" to make a dramatic breakthrough. There are
special moments akin to critical learning stages in a child

when everything is ready—psychologically, biologically and spiritually—for a leap forward in one's growth. When all of these elements come together, then a family reconstruction can be extraordinarily powerful.

To begin building warmth and trust in small groups (not with groups of 30 or more) I invite participants to give their names, what they are feeling, and what brought them to the group. I share my feelings first to model what I mean by my instructions and to allow the members to identify with me.

Next I break the group into dyads, asking the participants to pair up with someone they don't know, to sit together and close their eyes. I ask them to be aware, with their eyes closed, of what they are feeling and thinking. Giving them plenty of time to do this, as it takes time to identify feelings, I then invite them to open their eyes and share with each other what they became aware of. Then in the group I ask what the experience was like for them.

There are several reasons for this exercise and I believe they are all important. First, being in pairs offers the most trusting modality there can be. Thus, it is the best format for building trust in the group. Second, there is no better way to share oneself with another than to tell what one is aware of feeling and thinking. All I have to offer a person at any given moment is myself—and what am I besides my body, thoughts and feelings? So I invite them to share that, not what they do for a living, or how many children they have, or what they expect for the day. I leave the direction very general so they can be responsive to whatever is going on inside of them.

Third, by having participants concentrate on what they are feeling I am asking them to be aware of the most hidden aspect of themselves. Most people quickly become aware of what thoughts are floating through their heads. Some are not adept at recognizing feelings. So this direction helps them identify emotions. Being aware of one's feelings will be a task constantly called for by the Guide throughout the reconstruction. To call for this in the very first exercise begins to sharpen that skill and emphasize its importance.

Fourth I ask that participants close their eyes, thus cutting off one of our most important ways of functioning. With this faculty taken away, one is immediately cast into an altered way of being. This heightens awareness of one's internal state. Taking away the power to be in contact with the outside world—by seeing what's out there—helps a person to go inside to see what is there instead.

Fifth, sharing with a partner is an experience in self-expression, an experience of one's power and self-completion, an experience of wholeness. Since we are by nature expressive creatures, we are not experiencing ourselves completely until we do express ourselves.

After this first exercise, I then do several others within the same dyads. And after each dyadic sharing I will ask for feedback in the large group: What did they discover? How was it for them? Moving back and forth between the dyadic and group experience builds trust in the larger group as well as within the dyads. As people experience safety in sharing with one, they can share with more. Maintaining this balance between expressing oneself in the dyad and in the group is important. It also models the way life can be in general—a movement from being with self (close your eyes and . . .) to being with one other (share with your partner) to being with three or more (share in the group). All of life is lived within those modalities. Each has its own unique role to play in enhancing human development.

I want to take this opportunity to explain briefly how critical it is for growth that there be this balance in life between being alone, with one other, and with two or more. Sometimes the major problem with clients of mine will be the failure to have these three modalities functioning effectively in their lives.

Being alone and entering deeply into the inner self, reflecting upon one's experiences and allowing one's unconscious to emerge into consciousness, is the only way I know of to deepen oneself and integrate one's experience. This is why meditation, reflection and contemplation have been advocated by wise people throughout the ages. It amazes me how so many never allow this quiet and aloneness to happen to them as they constantly bombard themselves with external stimuli.

Being with one other in the intimacy of trust and openness is the only way that seems to allow a person the fullness of self-expression. At the same time, it is also the only modality that allows a person to receive another person as completely as possible. To express ourself and to receive some feedback is a basic need of the human species and is the richest kind of learning, growth and expansion of experience.

However great being alone and being with just one other are, these are not enough for a full human life. Being in a threesome or more adds another human dimension, namely the ability to receive confirmation of one's identity and humanness. This is experienced when the dyads report to the larger group what they were experiencing, and people feel confirmed when they see that others besides their partner experienced the same thing. Or even better, this confirmation occurs when the partner in the dyad did not experience the same as the person. At that point the person can say, "If my partner didn't experience the same as I, am I weird or something?" When that person, in the larger group, finds several others with the same experience, then confirmation of one's humanness and identity takes place. The triadic experience is also one in which differences or disagreements can be resolved. The necessity of this modality is behind such processes as mediation, arbitration, marriage counseling, and the Camp David accords.

So in building trust and a rich human experience in the family reconstruction group, I try to maintain a balance between the three modalities of human existence: being alone (close your eyes and be in touch with what is going on inside you), being with one other (now share what you became aware of with your partner), and being with three or more (let's return to the large group and share the experience).

The exercises I give to the dyads after the first one are designed to help the members think in a family systems way. Some of the exercises are as follows:

1) Picture your father before you. Identify what you liked the most about him and what you disliked the most. Share with your partner. Do the same exercise with your mother.

2) As you see your father and mother, picture how your father basically related to your mother, and how your mother related to your father. Share this with your partner. What would you have liked to see changed in the way each related to the other?

3) What are three prominent characteristics of your father? Of your mother? Which of these do you think you picked up from them? Share your thoughts with your partner.

4) What one thing would you have wished were different in the way your mother (father) related to you?

This gives you a taste of the kind of exercises I lead the participants through. They touch upon dynamics that will very likely be dealt with in the ensuing family reconstruction. I continue with these exercises until I feel the group is close together. If the group is brand new, it might take some two hours from the opening introduction to the completion of two or more exercises.

BONDING THE EXPLORER WITH THE GROUP

Although the Guide has previously interviewed the Explorer, it is important that the Explorer be interviewed again after group trust has been developed. Since that interview the Explorer may have had new insights, perhaps even a new agenda for the family reconstruction. Being in the group setting arouses its own particular reactions in the Explorer. These reactions need to be identified and expressed. Are there any fears, hesitations? What does the Explorer want from the group? Perhaps the Explorer will feel embarrassed that the family reconstruction will be dull or that it won't mean much to the group.

Sometimes the Explorer is shy about having an entire day spent in his behalf, as if he were unworthy of so much attention. Maybe the Explorer fears what people will think of his family. Often I ask the group to express their reactions to the fears, hesitations, wonderings of the Explorer. When the Explorer hears from the members, he is often reassured and relieved.

Again, the entire contract is renewed before the group— what the Explorer wants to accomplish, what his or her current dilemmas are, what is expected from the Guide and the group, and what the Guide expects from the Explorer. Thus, the group and the Explorer are bonded by both their mutual sharing of themselves and a common understanding of the goals of the family reconstruction.

Then I explain role playing to the group. Often some participants are anxious about this—thinking that they must be actors and actresses of some skill. Being a role player is not acting at all. It is not like reading a script and trying to imagine what the character is like so as to imitate him in some way. Role players are to be just themselves and allow whatever thoughts and feelings come to them. I invite them to trust the process and just be themselves.

The process consists of two elements. First the Explorer picks people to play the family members whom they resemble in some way. This is done mainly out of the unconscious part of the Explorer. The Explorer many times cannot give reasons for the choices made. Yet in my experience almost always the choices are surprisingly ''correct.''

The second element is the way the role players will be

enrolled. The Explorer places the role players in a statue-like position (sculpting) that represents the way the Explorer pictures that person in relation to the other people in the family. By staying frozen for a minute or two, the role player begins to get feelings and thoughts. When the role player shares those thoughts and feelings, the Explorer is usually amazed at how that resembles the real family member. I also ask the Explorer to speak directly to the character in the here and now, discussing their relationship. (For example: ''Dad, you are always reading and none of us kids can talk to you. We would like to because you are a nice guy but forbidding in some way. You work hard. I don't think you and Mom get along too well, though you never argue before us. You aren't affectionate with her in front of us. You love to go fishing and are very close to two of your fishing buddies. I often wished you'd take me fishing.'')

As the role players begin to go through certain scenes, they become powerfully enrolled into the personalities they represent. As the drama unfolds, other reactions automatically occur. There is no need to force anything. To force an attitude or way of being, to try to act, only diminishes the process and effect.

Sometimes the Explorer will be afraid to choose a person to play the role of a despicable character, or a group member will be affronted to be chosen to play such a person. To forestall that I will deliberately raise this issue if I feel it may occur. I point out that in every negative trait lies the seed of a positive, and vice versa. For example, while one may dislike Richard Nixon's cunning, in that trait there is the seed of fierce determination and the capacity to survive. A classic blamer and put-down artist has within that negative trait the seed of knowing what one wants and using power to defend oneself. The placator has the positive seed of being sensitive to other people and their needs. Being lazy has in it the capacity of being relaxed and a kind of acceptance of life as it is. The positive trait of being gentle has the seed of being weak; strength has the seed of being pushy or domineering. Part of the growing process is to transform the negatives into positives by using the positive seed embedded in each negative.

So, in a family reconstruction, we will see just such characters and the dynamics. Because of this each person playing a role has the opportunity to learn how a positive trait could become a negative one and vice versa. In the role playing a person may discover what is required to develop the positive seed present in any negative trait.

It is beneficial for the Explorer as well as for the group to be told how the group members can gain from the day. In fact, I have seen a member of a group gain more from a family reconstruction then the Explorer. The family portrayed often bears a remarkable similarity to a group member's family. In playing a role, a participant can get new insights that help him understand both himself and his family better. The role players can see for the first time what is needed to be able to change themselves and their family systems.

The Explorer benefits from this explanation, realizing that there can be great gains for others from the family reconstruction. Helping the members gain for themselves can be facilitated by a little exercise that can be done at the beginning of the day. I ask the participants to close their eyes and be aware of a current dilemma in their lives; then to picture the family they grew up in; then to be aware of any puzzles or questions that come to them. After giving them sufficient time for this, I invite them to be open to getting some answers or insights from this day by being open to what is happening to them. At the end of the family reconstruction, I again ask group members to close their eyes and recapture their dilemma, family and puzzles, and then to see if the family reconstruction has added anything relevant to their dilemma and questions.

In an ongoing family reconstruction group, individual members get on a roll, as it were, and every family reconstruction becomes a new step for them in their own personal development.

After the group warmup, the interview with the Explorer, and necessary explanations, the group is poised and ready —after a short break—to begin choosing the role players.

5 THE JOURNEY BEGINS

Once trust has been established in the group and we know the personal aims of the Explorer, the process of choosing role players begins. This is a critical step. If the Explorer makes appropriate choices, he or she will have chosen people who resemble his or her family members in remarkable ways. This step, plus proper enrollment as described in Chapter 6, will almost guarantee a successful journey for the Explorer.

As the Explorer picks people for the roles, I help the unconscious part of the Explorer come into full play. By the time we have arrived at this point in the family reconstruction, the Explorer is usually already operating from an altered state of consciousness. All members of the group have gone through exercises inviting them to "slow down." They have closed their eyes to discover their internal state of feelings and thinking, to be aware of their breathing, and to be more sensitive than normally to their feelings. The Explorer is "up" and in a state of anticipation. Being in an altered state, the Explorer's unconscious can operate more fully.

As I ask the Explorer to stand with me and carefully look around the room to pick someone to be his mother, I invite him to take each person in with his eyes. If the Explorer has difficulty choosing, I tell him to let the person pick him by being a magnet drawing the Explorer to choose him or her. If the Explorer tends to be a fast decider, I will deliberately slow down the decision process; if he is a slow decider, I will quicken the process. I do this in order to encourage the person to function not in his or her ordinary manner but from an altered state.

By this time I will know if the Explorer is a fast or slow decider, a quick or slow thinker. It seems that some people deal with information by primarily visualizing the data, some by feeling the data, and some by hearing the data. For example, when I'm introduced to a new person I need to ask how the name is spelled. Being visually oriented, I get a picture of the spelling in my imagination and then I can remember it. Some people never need to do this. As soon as they hear the name, they have it and can repeat it accurately from then on.

If I detect that the Explorer is primarily visual, I will ask him to get a *feel* for the person he is choosing for his mother. If he feels information, I'll ask him to *see* his mother in the crowd or tune in to her. I invite the person to choose from the mode that is not ordinarily his to use. Thus, he is encouraged to operate in an altered state. This also helps activate the unconscious.

Sometimes, in the role-choosing process I will interfere in different ways. I remember that when one man chose someone to be his alter ego I immediately had a gut feeling that he had picked a person most unlikely to be a good stand-in. Instead of challenging the man to choose someone else (I would rather go sideways with resistance), I asked him to pick from the group the *least* likely person to play his alter ego. I then had both persons act as the alter ego during the family reconstruction. It was a wise move. As the day evolved, the least likely person had reactions that were also in the Explorer but deeply covered within his psyche. The first choice of alter ego offered little new to the Explorer as the day proceeded. The second choice enabled the Explorer to open up to the hidden motives, feelings and perceptions that until then had been too threatening to admit. The first choice represented the Explorer on the conscious level and the second choice represented the Explorer on the unconscious level.

In another family reconstruction (the second I did with Linda, two years or so after I had done her first one), I asked her to pick her alter ego. Early in the morning she had mentioned that she had invited a friend of hers to come to the group as this friend had the same emotional and mental problem. Linda described non-connected thoughts and experiences rapidly rushing through her brain until she thought she was going crazy. Linda's friend, Bobbie, who had the same problem, talked at length at the beginning of the group session about her problem and how scary that experience was. Both women had been diagnosed as having "brain allergies" and were on strict diets to reduce the phenomenon of speeding thoughts. Linda was still fearful of going out of control.

When Linda picked Mary as her alter ego, I invited her to think again. She said she could also pick Barbara, that she was torn between the two. I asked her why she didn't pick her friend Bobbie. She immediately and forcefully rebelled against this idea. The rejection was so strong that I felt Linda was protecting herself by not picking her friend. It was as though she would not accept a person with the very same traits. I spent two hours working with Linda over this issue. At last she chose her friend. The major breakthrough of this family reconstruction was completed in the very choosing of the alter ego—Linda allowed herself to accept herself! Linda's non-acceptance of self was a more important issue for her than her fear of the rushing brain phenomenon. Once she accepted herself—chose her friend as her alter ego—she seemed to be able to deal with her fear of going crazy. What followed in the rest of the family reconstruction helped Linda understand from her family system how she had become so non self-accepting and how to deal with this problem in better ways.

I usually ask the Explorer to pick the role players of parents and alter ego first. Often I guide the Explorer to choose his alter ego first, especially if I think that choice is more important than mother or father. I might even ask the Explorer to choose another family member before mother or father if I feel that other member is more significant in the reconstruction process. Sometimes, for example a grandparent is more important, especially if the parent is practically the clone of the grandparent. I do this to allow the Explorer to pick the most appropriate person from the limited number in the group. I want that role player to have the instincts and the ways of feeling and perceiving closest to the family member being played. Those chosen for the roles of alter ego, mother and father will stay in those roles for the entire family reconstruction. They will play no other roles than those.

After these most important people are picked, I ask the Explorer to pick members of the maternal or paternal family, depending upon which family is to be reconstructed first. People playing roles of the paternal family can also play parts of the maternal family. Many times I choose to first develop the side of the family known least by the Explorer. The most unknown side of the family may take more time and energy.

If the Explorer draws nearly a complete blank concerning the side of the family unknown to him, then I will develop the side that is known. As the known side is developed, the Explorer can unconsciously be getting a sense of what the other family might look like. For example, the Explorer who knows the father's family well may perceive the father's parents as rigid taskmasters raising the father to be the same. From this knowledge, added to the few threads of unconscious knowledge concerning the mother's family, the Explorer may appropriately perceive mother's parents as relaxed, fun-loving people. A woman coming from this atmosphere would be an appropriate choice for a rigid type of man.

Sometimes I will first develop the side that seems more important to me in terms of unraveling the mystery surrounding the Explorer's dilemma. For example, if the Explorer has unresolved problems of anger and hatred with his father, I might develop the father's side first, even though it is better known than the mother's side. However, the more I understand family systems, the more I see that what might be more crucial for the Explorer to see is how the mother contributed to the Explorer's anger. Sometimes the Explorer is secretly more angry at the mother than at the father. So from this viewpoint it would be better to develop the mother's side first.

In one family reconstruction the Explorer, John, had an "irresponsible father, George, who drank too much, gambled too much and never held a job of any worth." Thus the mother, Connie, "was forced to go to work to earn the livelihood for the family." In John's eyes George was a failure and Connie was the hero. John was raised to be a helping sort of lad, very reliable, who seldom was allowed to show anger, especially toward any superior or parent. John came to the family reconstruction with a quiet, suffused anger toward his father, which was expressed by a cold indifference. In fact, several years before, John had been called by Connie to help solve the growing menace of his father's drinking, which she said might lead to "his burning down the house with his cigarettes while I'm off working." The only solution Connie and John could think of was to put him away in a state hospital since his drinking was incurable. That seemed logical at the time and, given the circumstances, may have been the only viable solution.

However, the reconstruction showed that Connie really maneuvered to have the decision to institutionalize George made primarily by John rather than by Connie, who was quite competent to make such a decision. In fact, John's sister was never consulted because, as John said, "She would have never gone along with it."

Due to several other ensuing events, John began to resent his mother for dumping this load on him, although

John was totally unaware of this until the reconstruction. Then John realized that much of the suppressed anger directed at his dad was really aimed at his mom. This reality was slow to emerge since John had difficulty being overtly angry to begin with! Once it became clear during the reconstruction that John really did have stores of suppressed anger at his mother, he was able to express it. Thus he freed up lots of energy that he was using to protect his image of his hero mother. His case is, then, a good example of how anger directed toward a father can actually be anger toward the mother.

As the Explorer picks people to play the roles of all the members of a family, it is important for him or her to choose players for stillborn and miscarried babies. These children often are critical to what evolves in a family. They can deeply affect the way mothers and fathers feel about themselves and each other. They can set a pattern that influences children who come after such events. It is also important to have the Explorer choose people to play roles of all the people living in the home during the formative years such as grandparents, aunts, cousins or even hired hands. This is true in each of the three families enacted during the day.

As the members of the group are chosen to play the different roles, each prints the name of the character on masking tape and wears it as long as he or she is in the role. This process goes on until all family members and live-ins (especially in-laws) are chosen for the three families: the Explorer's family, and the Explorer's mother's and father's families. We are now ready to move into the next important step, enrolling the players.

6 THE STORY OF ONE JOURNEY INTO LIGHT

In order to describe how a family reconstruction unfolds, I will describe the actual reconstruction of a 37-year-old woman whom I shall call Ann. Ann did her family reconstruction because she wanted to heal her relationship with her mother. All through her life Ann had felt threatened by and encroached upon by her mother. She also perceived her mother as being somewhat crazy, off-the-wall at times. She wated some understanding of why her mother had acted and continued to act in this way. On the other hand, Ann had had a loving relationship with her father, feeling compassion and empathy for him. He could do no wrong while mother could do nothing right.

Before interviewing Ann I read her homework. Two things were noteworthy. One was Ann's closing observation that she felt like she was "caught up in mud." She felt a great deal of pain, was terribly afraid, and felt revulsion at the thought of going back into her history and revisiting all the past painful experiences. She had done a great deal of work in dealing with her depression and the dysfunctional aspects of her life—retraining herself, as it were. She was afraid that if she worked at this past again it would undo all of her training.

The second thing I noted was that she began the chronology at her own birth rather than with her grandparents' births. There was nothing at all in the chronology about her parents' being married or about her mother's or father's families, although the instructions were clear that she was to go back to those families. In response to the assignment on birth fantasies, she wrote that she simply could not fantasize anything about her mother's birth although she did the fantasies of her father's and her own births.

These two observations suggested that there would be a great deal of resistance within her to seeing any new pictures, so I decided to raise this issue with her during the interview. The way the family reconstruction was arranged, though, I did not have a chance to interview Ann prior to the time of the reconstruction. In the interview in the midst of the group, I did confront her about her fear of going back into the past. I was relieved to hear that this had been a momentary expression and that the fear wasn't great enough to prevent her from doing her family reconstruction. I then told her she might well not be able to get any new perceptions of her mother, nor any new feelings toward her. In fact, the old angry and hateful feelings had served her in some way. Perhaps those old perceptions and feelings had protected her. It might be too threatening for her to give that up. I told her I thought that would be okay; she might have to keep those old feelings for her own safety.

I think when I said that to her something was released within her; she became more open to something new happening for her in terms of her mother. I wonder how effective the family reconstruction would have been if I had not done this in the interview. As you will see, the family reconstruction was indeed very powerful and she did see her mother in a more compassionate, understanding and loving way. By giving her permission to keep the old pictures and feelings of her mother, she was free to go in either direction. It took the compulsiveness out of the whole dynamic.

Prior to beginning the interview, Ann had put large charts of her three genograms or family trees on a wall so everyone could refer to them. I include them here (Figures 12, 13, and 14).

understood her mother's motivations, that might not help.

Figure 12. Ann's father's family

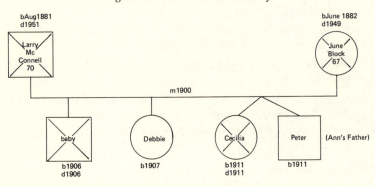

Ann seemed confused as to how she could find some reconciliation with her mother. I made the following points:

First, I said to Ann, ''Through the family reconstruction you might be able to see how your mother was simply doing the best she knew how, that she was trying to survive in some way. I believe that most acting-out comes from someone being under terrific stress, being threatened. This behavior is the way people protect themselves.

Figure 13. Ann's mother's family

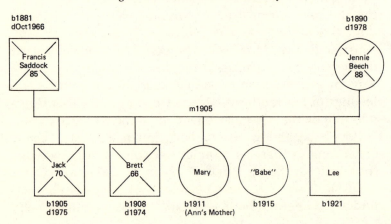

Figure 14. Ann's family

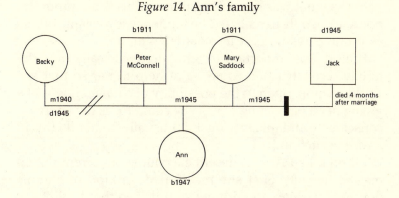

"However," I continued, "if it appeared that Mary, your mother, was just a good old hard-core egotistical, self-centered, insensitive person, it would be hard to have any soft, reconciling feelings toward her. It would be hard to see how she was doing the best she knew how and was acting out to protect herself. In going back to Mary's family and seeing how she was raised, you might get some insight into how she became a self-centered, egotistical person, and then your attitude toward your mother may begin to change."

Second, it is indeed very unlikely that her mother will ever come and say, "Hey, here are all the ways I offended you as you were growing up and I apologize." Ann had stated earlier that she wished for an apology from her mother. In fact, I told Ann, "Mary may be blind to how she was adversely affecting you. Blinding oneself to what one is doing is a good way of protecting oneself. It is very threatening to discover that one is really screwing up one's daughter. It is also possible that those around your mother participated in keeping her blind to what she was doing, including yourself! How often did you tell your mother your true feelings about what she was doing?"

Ann admitted that she had hidden most of her painful and angry feelings. She began to see how she had participated in what was happening to her. This is an important point for people to realize. The tendency is to blame others as if one plays no part in what is going on.

I felt it was important to tell Ann specifically how the family reconstruction could be of help to her so that she could be more open to the possibility of change. It was like giving her a path along which she could focus her energy—consciously and unconsciously. (I usually do not do this in a reconstruction.)

I then asked Ann to describe a couple of current dilemmas in her life. First she mentioned "a kind of chronic depression going on with me so much so that I call it my pet." This confirmed what she had said earlier about not expressing her anger toward her mother. Instead she was swallowing it, which led to chronic depression. She said that a second dilemma is that her mother is still trying to encroach upon her life. Then Ann returned to her depression, saying that it seemed to be getting worse. She did know some ways to pull herself up once in a while, but even these learned techniques weren't working for her these days.

I asked whether she ever confronts Mary when she tries to encroach upon her life. Ann said, "Well, not really. I just don't have the energy for that. I just kind of get cold and withdrawn, and maybe I call my father and complain to him about it." She said that recently she did get screamingly angry at her mother. "There were only about two other times in my life when I ever did this," she explained. "I don't get angry at Mother too often because this has a negative effect on Dad—he gets sick when I get angry at Mother."

Ann had learned from her father not to confront or show anger toward her mother. I pointed this out to Ann. I asked her if her mother encroached upon her father. She said that she really didn't know what went on between them. That suggested that she had never seen Peter get angry at Mary. I pointed out clearly to Ann how the role played by her father had had such an unhealthy impact on her. Ann had such an unrealistic view of her father as the good guy that I had to take every opportunity to balance that with some of his limitations, especially when they impinged on Ann. One of the main thrusts of a family reconstruction is to help the Explorer see the parents as real humans rather than as either gods or devils.

When we ended the interview I became more convinced that Ann judged on some unconscious level that she had to keep her hard view of Mary. If she softened, she would get close to Mary and then might be overwhelmed by her again. And because she was afraid to use her anger for fear of hurting her father, she never felt any power with Mary. Since Ann seldom experienced power with her mother, she felt threatened by the mere thought of getting close to her. I thought that in this family reconstruction I needed to help Ann feel strong with her mother as well as understand her in an empathic way. If I could let her express some anger and realize that her Dad would not wither away, then we might have a valuable experience. But I kept myself open to how the process would unfold.

I asked Ann to place her alter ego, the person she chose to play her role during the day, in a statue position that would illustrate how she sees herself today. Ann had seen this process, called sculpting, so she was able to do it. For beginners who have no idea what sculpting is, I simply sculpt someone myself. In this case I might show Ann a sculpt of her alter ego, illustrating how I see Ann this day. Sculpting is one of the most powerful ways to enroll a person to play a role in a family reconstruction. To help the Explorer create as accurate a likeness as possible, I ask the Explorer to check the eyes (where they are directed), the facial expression, the placement of the legs, the arms, hands and fingers—to look at every part of the body until the entire statue seems right.

If the Explorer does a lot of talking, I direct that the sculpt be made in silence. Usually talkers won't touch the body of another, won't move them around, change the hands, etc. If I can get the Explorer to make the sculpt in an altered way of behaving, this accesses the unconscious of the Explorer. It is in the unconscious that so much of the powerful information resides. The unconscious knows more than the conscious. Sculpting is a beautiful tool to get in touch with this source. This is why the results of sculpting are so accurate!

Ann sculpted her alter ego as shown in Figure 15. I told the alter ego to stand perfectly still in the sculpt. This creates thoughts and feelings. After a minute or two of silence, I asked the stand-in Ann to report what was going on inside her. She said that she was feeling tense around the shoulders, tense in her eyebrows, and that she was feeling perturbed, afraid, not knowing what was going to happen next. I asked Ann her reaction to this. She said that it really fit. "That's the way I feel about myself—disturbed and not sure what's going to happen next in my life," she said.

Then I asked Ann to sculpt her stand-in to represent how she would look if a miracle occurred. She sculpted her alter ego as in Figure 16. I asked the stand-in what she felt. She said, "I felt clean inside and real open to what is out there, full of hope and optimism, very hopeful about life." Ann really liked that.

This illustrates how powerful and accurate sculpting is. The sculpt that Ann made caused feelings and thoughts to occur in her alter ego that were identical to those Ann had in real life! Unless you have had this experience it will be hard for you to believe the process. If Ann had slightly altered her sculpt, it would produce different feelings and reactions. Even though I have seen this process work a thousand times, I am still amazed every time it happens!

There were several reasons I asked Ann to sculpt her alter ego into these two positions. First, it made Ann a believer in this process so that she would be open to what would happen throughout the reconstruction. In addition, I wanted her to see and appreciate how super it is to be different, even though it might take much time and effort to come to be as in the second sculpt. I guess I also wanted to test Ann's openness to the process; this was more in my unconscious than conscious awareness at the time. Further, I wanted to see if either Ann or her alter ego would somewhat naturally return to the open and hopeful second sculpt by the end of the family reconstruction.

I then asked Ann to sculpt her mother and father as she mainly saw them when she grew up; the result is shown in Figure 17. After staying frozen in the sculpt, they were asked what they were feeling and thinking. Mary reported that she felt lonely. She also felt some support from her husband, but she felt she had no contact with him other than support. I asked her what kept her from getting more contact. She said that she just couldn't move; she said she felt a great deal of hurt in not being able to make that connection.

Peter reported that he felt some detachment and discomfort because while he was looking at his wife she was not looking at him; however, he felt some warmth and positive feelings around the fact that he could put his hand on her shoulder and do some supporting of her. Peter also reported that something kept him from bending around and looking into his wife's eyes. So just as Mary felt that she couldn't move, so did Peter. I commented that some rule seemed to be operating in both of them that kept them from moving to get more from each other.

Normally I would at this point ask Ann what her reaction was to hearing all of this. But I didn't ask her. I wanted her to just take it in, for it was a new picture of her mother. I didn't want to give Ann a chance to say something expressing some rejection of her mother's being lonely. Such an expression might strengthen Ann's negative picture of her mother. I could see that Ann was surprised to hear what her mother and father said in her sculpt of them.

There are no rules saying that you set up a sculpt of the

Figure 15. Ann's alter ego as Ann sees herself at the beginning of the family reconstruction

Figure 16. Ann as she wants to be

Figure 17. Ann's mother and father as she saw them as she was growing up

parents' relationship to one another before you develop the families of mother and father. I asked Ann to do so because I wanted to see how the sculpt would look before it was influenced by unfolding of their separate families of origin. I just had a gut feeling that I should do it. Most of what I do comes out of my instinct and intuition as the scenes unfold. Sometimes I'm aware of why I do certain things and at other times I'm not.

I wanted to develop Peter's family next, mainly through sculpting. I was afraid of Ann's verbal description taking her too much into her conscious area, where everything was sweetness and roses concerning her father. Yet just from looking at the family tree I could tell that Peter's life was very complicated due to the deaths of his twin sister and a brother as infants. Very likely, Ann was unaware of the impact of these deaths upon her father's life.

When Ann picked the people to play June and Larry, I simply told them the information I had learned from the family tree: when and where they were born, and how long they lived. Then I immediately asked Ann to sculpt them as she fantasized the way they looked when they got married. I want to quote Ann's own words as she was doing this since they will show you how this method accesses the unconscious. Obviously Ann wasn't there when June and Larry got married, but as she sculpted and talked I could see how this scene became more and more real to Ann. Ann said to June: "You're almost in the right position except that you're too nice-looking in your face; you've got to be real stern, stern, stern. You're the woman who says, 'It would be better to die than get a case of syphilis.'" To Larry she said, "No, don't do that—straight up, straight and narrow. I don't know if you can do this or not—sort of a stern look but in the back of your mind you're thinking of this joke and you're just about ready to start laughing, but don't because you'll irritate her." Ann went back to June and said, "Stop biting your lips so much. Look stern with the righteousness of someone who knows that they're in the right. You don't have to clench your lips because you're right, and the rest of the world will know it someday. Yes, that's perfect.''

To give you the flavor of how keeping people in a sculpt brings forth feelings and thoughts, I will quote directly from the role players who portrayed June and Larry after they had been sculpted by Ann.

June: ''I am feeling rigid. I'd really like to relax my knees. It's making my back ache. Standing this way hurts my neck. It's a big sacrifice you make in order to be right.'' Sighs.

Larry: ''I'm feeling okay, have both feet on the ground. I'm feeling detached but taken care of. My investment here isn't real big, that's why I'm doing okay. I'm not having to work real hard at this. I do okay at my job and I feel pretty comfortable, but maybe a little lonely too, a little lonely from the detachment, sort of like a boarder in my own house. But there is no real problem so I'm not going to change anything.''

I then turned to Ann and asked her what her reaction was to hearing June and Larry. ''I think that is probably how he felt,'' she said. ''June died when I was real little, Larry died shortly after. I don't have any memories of her, but I do remember their house as being clean and shining, sparsely furnished with furniture of heavy dark wood, just everything clean and in its place. I just remember my mother saying June was real strict and stern.'' I then asked Ann what she was feeling. ''I don't have any feelings toward her since I didn't know her,'' Ann said. I asked if she had any feelings from the sculpt. Ann then said that she felt sad that there seemed to be so little joy and life in her father's family.

After this I told Larry and June that they were soon to have a baby. I gave June a rolled up sweater which she put under her blouse to show her pregnancy. It is important that these little touches be done so that the Explorer gets more and more drawn into the reality of the picture she is seeing. Also, small touches like this add humor; throughout the reconstruction I try to balance the heavy and serious with some light moments. I then asked Larry and June to report what happened when they noticed the pregnancy.

Larry: "I'm feeling pretty heavy-hearted. Getting pregnant, being pregnant is sort of a mechanical function just like the trains are. There is still no investment there. Real heavy, like here [points to his stomach]. It's like the jokes are a way of getting by. Take care of the house, you go to work and bring income, but there is a real heavy feeling."

From these reactions, Ann was beginning to sense the shape of the family into which her father is to be born.

I then told Larry and June that the time had come for them to have their baby. The sweater was removed from June's blouse and I put a pillow into June's arms. Then I picked up their reactions to the birth of this baby boy.

June: "What shall we name this baby?"

Larry: "I don't have any idea. You take care of these things. You can come up with a pretty good name."

June: "I feel scared. I'm afraid. Let's don't tell anybody. Do you want to hold him?"

Larry: "Oh no, no, it's okay."

Then I told them that in a week or two the baby died. To represent this I turned the pillow over.

June: "It's my fault. I didn't know what to do with the baby. I didn't know how to take care of a baby. I just looked at the baby; I didn't know what to do. It's all my fault. I wasn't a good enough person. I tried so hard."

Larry: "It's okay, we'll have another one."

June: "I'll make it up to you."

I asked them what they were feeling inside that they were not saying.

Larry: "I'm standing here and sort of involuntarily rocking. I started doing that and not realizing I was doing it. The time the pregnancy was going on I started realizing that I'm holding one hand behind my back and my right hand is holding my left hand. When the baby was born I wanted to reach out to the baby but my hands were tied; even though it was being offered for some reason my hands stayed tied. I don't understand that. I don't know what's going on, but I think that's what happened.''

June: ''My feeling was the same as his. I wanted to love the baby but I was afraid to. I went through a hell of a lot to get this baby, and here he comes out a little bitty thing. It isn't anything like I thought it was going to be. I kind of resent this baby and I feel very guilty now that he is dead.''

I then asked June and Larry to bury the baby. They laid the pillow down on the floor and looked very sad, kneeling before the baby on the floor. Then I asked them if there was anything they wished to say.

June: ''If we have another baby, I'll make up for this one.''

Larry: ''Well, I'm just gonna have to work harder, I'm gonna have to. I just didn't have things very well taken care of this time. We'll be better next time. I'll just work harder.''

June: ''You mean at your job?''

Larry: ''Work harder.''

June: ''At being away from home?''

Larry: ''I don't know. Work harder.''

When June heard him repeat he had to work harder she mumbled some derogatory comment. I asked her if she would have said that out loud and she said, ''Oh, no.'' I asked, ''Do you think you would have any conversation at home about another baby?'' Both said there probably wasn't any conversation, that it would just be presumed that they would go ahead and have another baby.

The next year June got pregnant and gave birth to their second child, a girl they named Debbie. I again put the folded sweater under June's blouse and asked her to share what she was thinking as she was pregnant with her second child.

June: ''This is going to be a perfect baby; I'll make this baby perfect.''

Larry: ''I am really nervous and I think I want to be more

active with this baby. I'm not real sure how I'm going to go about it.''

Then I invited the baby to be born with this grand destiny! At this point the person playing Debbie crawled out from between her mother's legs and propped herself up in front of her mother and father.

June: ''I am just overwhelmed. This is a real person, a real person. I'm going to show her that she is going to behave. She is going to be good 'cause I'm not gonna let God take this one away from me.''

At this point the baby scampered away from her mother. She was afraid of her mother.

To accelerate the process I then announced that Debbie was now five years old. I asked the role players to put themselves into a sculpt that seemed fitting, being aware of their feelings after living with each other for five years. June is 30 years old now, and Larry is 32; the next pregnancy is about due. In the sculpt, Larry is patting Debbie on the head. Larry then described an amazing reaction he had while petting Debbie on the head: he could feel important as a father as long as he treated Debbie in such a way as to make her helpless. He then would have some role to play in the family.

Ann blurted out with great exclamation that her dad treats her in a way that keeps her helpless so that he feels important about himself! ''He must have learned that from his dad! Grandpa McConnell also treats me the same way!'' So often in a family reconstruction an Explorer will see a pattern of behavior transmitted from one generation into the next. Often the Explorer sees how she or he is doing the very same thing. When this is seen the motivation to change is intensified.

When June's time arrived, she delivered twins. She was delighted that God had given her two babies. She felt affirmed in God's eyes at long last after having lost the first child. But then, about three weeks after the birth, the first of the twins (a girl) died. June then grabbed onto the remaining twin, Peter (Ann's father), and clutched him desperately, making sure that he would not die. When I asked Peter, June and Larry to report what was going on, Larry said he felt really good because he had Debbie, and June now had Peter. The pressure was off of him and he felt a little more connected to June. June said that she felt good at having the twins but then shocked when the little girl died. She became very desperate to make sure that Peter would not die.

Peter: "In the first couple of weeks, when my twin was alive, I felt very warmly received and gently touched. I felt good all over. As soon as my sister died and Mother clutched me, I felt trapped and felt that my world was cut off because I was grabbed in such a way that my vision was curtailed. So the gentle, warm, open feeling changed into one of feeling trapped."

Ann then stated that she remembered her father saying one time how much Ann's mother was like his own mother. "My Dad told me how surprised he was at this because he spent his life trying to get away from the clutches of his mother, June, and yet ended up marrying a woman very much like June who in turn clutches onto me," Ann said. Ann was amazed that even when you know you don't want to have someone like your mother, you end up with that kind of personality anyway in marriage.

Then, with a soft tone in her voice, Ann said to June, "I am feeling sad for you in losing your two babies, particularly since they meant to you that you were okay with God again."

June said that she felt rather helpless in knowing how to love the children. June felt that she couldn't admit this because that would be a sign of weakness. So she never told her husband her feelings of inadequacy.

I asked Ann what she was feeling. Ann felt two things toward June. "I felt empathy for you but also anger toward you," Ann told June. "Stop being so rigid, take a risk, reach out and try something, don't be so tied down by having to be perfect or to know it all."

At this point I invited Ann to close her eyes and to picture her father in front of her. "Be aware that your father excuses himself by blaming his mother for the way he was raised," I said. "Be aware that you are willing to confront June but not your father."

"I can't because it will hurt him," Ann replied.

I then told Ann that just as Peter didn't confront his mother, so she was not confronting her father.

Letting that rest in Ann, I then turned to the family and invited the four of them to sculpt themselves when Peter was five and Debbie ten. When they formed the sculpt (Figure 18), what emerged was that Debbie moved over to protect Peter from his mother. Peter experienced this as being dominated by Debbie. Debbie wanted him to be one way and June wanted him to be another way. He was now dominated by two women. This could be a clue to how Peter could later marry a strong woman who might have a tendency to dominate him. Peter reported that he was feeling some

Figure 18. Peter, June, Debbie and Larry when Peter is five and Debbie is ten

anger toward his dad for not taking more initiative with June
to get her off his back. We ended the work with Peter's family at this point. I invited Peter to stay in touch with the way
he was feeling and thinking so that he would remember
what kind of a guy this family was influencing him to become.

I then turned to Ann's alter ego and asked her to share
what was going on with her. She told Ann that she saw a
pattern. Just as Peter grew up feeling helpless with his
mother, so Peter felt helpless with his wife, Mary. Also, she
saw Peter's resentment toward Debbie because Debbie had
a closer connection with her dad than he did. Ann admitted that all this was true. She now saw how her father was
passive. She acknowledged that her father feels so much
resentment toward Debbie that they haven't spoken to each
other for about 30 years! This break occurred at the death
of Grandpa McConnell. "When Gramps died he made Peter
the executor of the will and Debbie felt that she should have
been the executor," Ann said. "That led to a falling out that
lasted these 30 years. Perhaps the resentment that Peter felt
toward Debbie while growing up was simply bearing fruit
now."

A flash came to me. I asked the four role players to re-
sume the sculpt that they were just in and I substituted Ann
for her father, Peter. I let her remain in the sculpt until she
began to get internal reactions to it. I then had Debbie and
June share what they were thinking and feeling.

June said to (Ann) Peter: "Oh, you are the joy of my life
and you mean everything to me."

Debbie told (Ann) Peter: "Get away from her [June]."

This pattern of speech was repeated by June and Debbie.
Finally Ann, playing the role of Peter, screamed out: "I need
to leave, get out of this mess!"

I then asked Peter, who had been on the sideline watching, to share his thoughts. He said that the anger he originally had toward his father for not taking more initiative with

73562

June was completely covered by the barrage coming from the two women. So it was easy for him to see that he would never have been aware of the anger that he felt for his father.

Ann now began to be open to the fact that while she had looked upon her father with such glowing feelings, perhaps there could be some anger in her toward him for not taking greater initiative to protect her from her mother's intrusiveness. Next I invited Ann *to do* or say whatever was inside of her as she was in the sculpt. All she did was to shout out: "I want to get out of here." She stayed in the sculpt and did not move. I then pointed out to Ann that my instructions to her were "*to do* or say" what she wanted, but all she did was stay stuck in that position and scream out. She was amazed that she never thought to actually leave!

We then moved on to develop the family of Mary, Ann's mother. After Ann picked the role players, I invited her to sculpt the family. The ease and facility with which Ann moved in and sculpted the characters made me feel confident that she was really operating out of her unconscious as well as conscious mind. She made many adjustments in setting it up until it really seemed to be satisfying and fitting. The sculpture is shown in Figure 19. Upon looking at the picture you can see that her mother was pulled in many different directions by her family. Mary reported that she felt confused and out of control.

At this point I noticed that Ann was not getting caught up in what was happening even though the role players were reporting their reactions. Ann was not emotionally moved. So I decided to ask Ann to be each member of the family by getting into each one's sculpt, and then to carry on a dialogue with her mother. This worked! She became very enthusiastic as she played each character in the family. She played each character quite differently and, as a result, got into the spirit of what this family was like. Ann got constant feedback from Mary, her mother, as she played

Figure 19. Mary torn by all her family

each character. This brought Ann into deep emotional contact with her mother, enabling her to experience her mother in an entirely different light than she had when growing up under her dominance.

To give you a sense of how Ann worked, I will quote her dialogue verbatim as she played the role of Lee, the youngest child in the family. ''Babe and I are going down to the tracks. We're gonna put pennies on the tracks and let trains flatten them. And after that we are going out to old Jones's farm and take one of his horses and tie hay onto it and run the horse over his front yard so that hay is messed up all over it. After that we thought we'd take a ride down to the old store and steal some apples from the grocery man and just in general kind of mess things up. And you can go if you want. Oh, all right, don't go then.'' Lee was obviously a playful risk-taker and Mary couldn't see herself having this fun even though down deep she craved it.

After Ann finished playing the part of each family member, I invited all the players to get back into the original sculpt. I asked Mary to close her eyes and be in touch with what was going on inside. She said that besides feeling confused and helpless she felt something stuck in her throat and felt very sick.

Then I asked Ann to close her eyes and be in touch with what was going on inside her. After a minute or two she opened her eyes and said to Mary, "I now understand why you didn't want to have a large number of children when you got married, having been bombarded in this family. I feel sad that you had to pretend or act like one thing on the outside but have different feelings and thoughts going on in the inside. I'm sorry that you could never break through that and be yourself. You could never go off with Babe and Lee and enjoy yourself. You had to be the good girl, the right person as it were."

After that I invited Ann's alter ego to share what was going on with her. The alter ego reported that she could understand that Mary felt confused and helpless in this family, that Mary probably never did understand her own true unique self and personality.

Then I asked Mary to share what was going on with her after hearing both Ann and Ann's alter ego. Mary said: "It is really great to know that there is someone out there who really understands what is going on inside of me. It is like the first time that anyone really understood what was going on inside of me." The fact that in this psychodrama Ann's mother stated how marvelous it was to feel that someone understood her implanted in Ann's mind the importance of her giving her mother a deeper understanding in real life.

I invited Ann to speak directly to her mother. Ann said: "I'm glad that you feel good about being understood. I didn't realize that you weren't understood and how important that is to you, and I'm happy for you now.'' She said this in a very tender and compassionate tone of voice. I ended the work with this family by asking each of the role players if they had anything further they would like to share while still in role.

Since I was doing this reconstruction on a Saturday afternoon and the following Sunday morning, I ended Saturday evening by deroling the role players. Later I will explain the necessity of this process and how I do it.

7 THE JOURNEY NEARS THE LIGHT

The next morning, as we resumed the family reconstruction, Ann reported that she saw on a deeper level that she had not been allowed to express any negative feelings in her family; rather, she was expected to always be a happy person. Any expression of unhappy feelings would hurt her parents; they would feel that in some way they were not good parents since they believed that good parents produce happy kids and bad parents produce unhappy kids.

I asked Ann's role-playing parents, Peter and Mary, if they had any hunches about the origin of this prohibition against negative feelings. Peter said he could really see where this came from. Since his parents lost two children, he felt an enormous pressure to make them happy by being the perfect, happy kid. Thus, he incorporated this meaning and then passed it on to his family after he married Mary.

Mary said that as a child she was unhappy on the inside but acted happy on the outside. She decided that when she had a child she would make sure that her child was truly a happy child rather than unhappy as she had been, so there would be a lot of pressure on the child to "be happy." Mary also said that at the end of the sculpting the day before, she had seen a sadness in Ann's eyes and wanted to reach out and touch her, but something kept her from doing it. Something strange was holding her back so that she couldn't reach out.

At this point Ann began to cry and said, "That's really sad, that's exactly what she would have said to me."

Mary said that the reason she couldn't reach out and tell Ann, "Look, release your pain, don't keep it hidden like I do," was that if she did then she, Mary, would be releasing her own pain. Since she had kept that in so long it would be too threatening for her now to take the risk of shedding some of her own interior pain.

In this very tender and sad moment I was able to emphasize that just as Ann found it difficult to express her negative feelings in her family, so her mother had the same experience in her family. Maybe she could now understand her mother a lot better because in this way Ann herself was like her mother. This deepened Ann's ability to empathize with her mother and to see her mother in a new light. Ann stated that she definitely didn't want to carry on this kind of behavior anymore.

Before we had begun this Sunday morning session, I had asked each person to share his or her feelings. Everyone was upbeat. Ann was the last to speak. She announced that she was not feeling good. She had some sadness about her parents, and felt some shakiness. I pointed out to Ann that in fact she was already breaking her rule. In spite of everyone being up and happy she had had the courage to reveal that she was feeling just the opposite! We spent several minutes discussing this new behavior on the part of Ann. She said, "All right, now I've done it once, what do I do now?"

I invited her to appreciate herself for having done it—just to stay with that, and then to realize if she did it once today she could do it tomorrow and, if need be, the next day. Taking time, speaking slowly and letting her have some moments of silence to reflect on all of this helped to deepen the experience for her and to deepen her good feelings about herself over having done this.

I then began to work with Ann's parents, Peter and Mary. In order to help Peter and Mary get back into role, as well as to inform several new people in the group, I asked Peter and Mary to tell the group who they were and what they were like.

First we heard from Peter: "I'm Peter. I'm Ann's dad, and something you might want to know about me is that I'm sort of quiet and passive to what went on here. A lot of times I'm a person who might be misread because I might look one way on the outside but something quite the opposite may be going on inside. In my family I really learned how to keep my feelings and sort of stay out of situations just to survive because I had people tugging at me. My mom wanted me to be perfect. She had good intentions, she really wanted me to be okay. My sister was always trying to change me and trying to give me advice. She was older, and she just made my life hell. I still, to this day, can't stand her; we haven't spoken in many years, so it's a real bad situation. And my dad? Well, I'm a lot like him in some ways because he didn't talk about how he felt very much and that seemed to work for him, and I guess it worked for me too. I guess when I was looking for a wife, what I wanted was somebody who would be there to keep things sort of smooth, somebody I could really respect, somebody who would get the job done as far as keeping things peaceful so I could do my work."

I then asked Ann to share her reaction to what she just heard from her father. Ann said: "Well, I guess he did pick somebody who knew how to take care of things so that he could get his work done, and I guess she might look like she was strong. She acts real tough. I don't think she is that strong, but she definitely puts up a good front. She did know how to do domestic stuff."

I asked Mary to speak to the group. She speaks from her experiences of Saturday, some of which I did not describe in Chapter 6. She said: "Today I am 72. I am a dependable person, I had a lot of practice in my family. I had to take care of my father's needs and my older brothers' needs. And yesterday my sense was I may have been sexually abused by all of them. But I couldn't tell anybody how hurt I was—no one knows how hurt I was—but I took care of that family. I took care of my older brothers, my father, my younger brother and younger sister. I felt like I was responsible for all of them and they could depend on me; as much as I wanted to run and hide I was there. I kept that in and probably forgot a lot about it. I thought I was going to have many children myself and do all the things that I wanted people to do for me. But I think it was different. I got frightened after having one child, saw how blocked I was, how afraid I am. It was harder than I thought after having one.''

I said to Mary: ''Have you ever known anyone who said, 'I was physically abused as a kid and I resolved that when I grew up I would never abuse my kids,' and then they find themselves abusing? Or people who didn't get affection and proper understanding from their parents and swore that when they had their kids they would give them plenty of affection and acceptance and understanding, and then didn't?''

Mary said she knew people like that.

I said, ''Do you have an explanation why that is so?''

She didn't.

Then I pointed out that we can become very clear about what we don't want to be but the problem is that we haven't had any model of how to be different. So if a child grew up in a home where affection was not shown or given, the child as an adult may say, ''I want to give affection,'' but having no modeling of that, the person doesn't know how to do it. That's how people get stuck. The kid who is abused doesn't want to be an abuser, yet he doesn't know any way of handling frustration other than striking out. I deliberately entered into this dialogue with Mary so that Ann could take this in and get a deeper understanding of and more compassion for her mother.

I then turned to Ann and said, ''What do you think about what I said?''

"I think that's right," she replied. "When I think about getting married and having kids, I definitely want them to have a different experience than I had, but my fear is that since I haven't learned how to do any different I wouldn't be able to do it—so I'm afraid of having kids." It is not surprising that Ann, 37 years old, had never been married.

Ann then commented upon how surprised she was when Mary reported that she had a sense that she had been sexually abused. Ann had always suspected that that had happened to her mother because her mother had such negative views on sex. And then Jack, the older brother, said that he too had the feeling the day before in the role playing that he might have sexually abused her. And then Mary said, "But in that role I couldn't say anything about that yesterday. Being in that role there was some rule about not talking about that." Everyone who had played roles in that family laughed as if expressing that indeed it was true. Again this shows how people can get caught up in roles and how there is a real correlation between what takes place in the role playing and what the Explorer knows about the reality of the family.

I again pointed out to Ann that if her mother had been sexually abused and couldn't talk about it, she had carried a terrible burden around with her all these years. It must have affected her attitude toward sex. I pointed this out to Ann because it was another avenue toward understanding and compassion. Then I asked Mary what kind of man she would look for to marry. She replied: "Someone who would be very kind and take me away from the family. . . . Because I was so overstimulated in the family I would look for someone who is quiet and not so needy."

I asked Ann to explain the details of Peter and Mary's brief marriages before Peter and Mary met each other. Then I asked Ann to tell us how Peter and Mary first met.

One of the scenes that is very important to see in psychodrama is the time when the mother and father of the Explorer first laid eyes on each other. She knew that her mother and father met for the first time at a university club dance in their home town, so we created the dance. Various members of the group played the parts of other couples and we sang some music of the era. Ann saw her mother and father, through the role playing, meet and exhibit the kind of shyness and interplay that usually takes place in such a situation. This scene is powerful because it allows the Explorer to see the sexually appealing side of each parent's personality and to see the fun-loving part of their parents come alive. This offers the Explorer a more human picture of her parents.

We recreated the meeting scene at the dance and also the scene the next day when Peter went to visit Mary at her home. I let this unfold to reveal humor, seriousness, shyness and all the normal human characteristics that are triggered during such scenes. What is so strikingly revealed is that the very basic personality traits that have been developed in the family of origin are played out during these scenes. For example, Mary was governed by her need to be a good girl, to be right, yet inside she had exciting and playful feelings that she hid because of a need to be perfectly correct in society. She learned this in her family, as we saw when Mary's family was sculpted.

One of the ways Mary expressed her exciting feelings was to learn to solo fly an airplane. This had taken place during World War II. In the dating episodes Peter made much of that and Mary revealed that he was the only man who really seemed to appreciate her flying. This made Peter very appealing to Mary.

After these dating scenes I asked just Peter and then Mary to close their eyes to see what was drawing them to each other and why they would want to marry each other. After they shared that, I asked them to set up a sculpture that would represent how they felt on their wedding day. This sculpture is shown in Figure 20.

I then asked Ann what she saw in their sculpture. She

Figure 20. Peter and Mary on their wedding day

said she saw two people very proud of each other, very much in love, obviously having common dreams and hopes —at which point Ann began to cry. I invited her to speak to her parents. She told them she wished she had known them at that time in their lives, that they appeared to be such warm, loving, good people—obviously not the couple she experienced as she was growing up. Seeing this side of her parents that she had never seen before touched Ann and moved her to tears. She told them that she felt she had somehow messed up their relationship, that she saw them so young and vital, having so much love for each other. She said this to them through her tears, in a very tender, loving way.

I then invited Ann to see if there was anything that she would like to express to her mother or father or *do* with her mother or father. Along with this invitation I told her that we were going to end the family reconstruction at this point. This was to motivate her to see if there was any final thing she wanted to say to her mother or father.

Ann, still in tears, told her mother how sorry she felt that her mother couldn't have had this kind of life throughout all these years of the marriage, and told her that she realized how she had to do the things that she did do later on. Then Ann embraced her mother in a very loving way; they stood there holding each other.

While that silent embrace was going on, I invited Ann to fantasize the moment of her birth and how her mother embraced her and touched her and took care of her when she was a baby. I did this because I wanted her to realize that just as she was feeling this tender love at this moment, that the same kind of tender love was most likely being afforded to her when she was a little baby. This is important because our beginnings are critical to our future, and how we conceive of ourselves at birth has a lot to do with our self-esteem.

Then Ann turned and gave a loving embrace to her father. When they separated, I had her sit down next to me and be silent. I let her absorb the experience; then I asked her if there was anything further she wished to do before we brought the reconstruction to a complete end. She said that she couldn't think of anything, at which point I said to her: ''I have a feeling that there probably are a lot of questions in your mind, like what happened in their marriage to turn it the way you experienced it. I think those are important questions. But I also feel that this experience we have right now is so important that I would like you to be patient with your processes and to allow these experiences to grow. This is all new for you—seeing your father and mother in a whole different way and with a fuller understanding of their dynamics. Stay with what you have now and you will have time later, as the months go on, to deal with other questions and issues around your mother and father.'' She seemed to be content with that, as if she really did want to stay with the new perceptions and understandings.

When I finished saying this I asked Ann's alter ego if she had anything to say. She told Ann how much she appreciated her strength in doing this and being open to what had happened during the two days, that she especially appreciated that Ann seemed to be open to changing her ways of dealing with her parents since she saw that the old ways weren't working for her.

I then invited any of the other role players to share whatever they needed to say from within their roles. Several of them did. Ann took in what they had to say with the same degree of openness that she had maintained during the family reconstruction. Most of the messages were loving messages to her.

When this was finished I proceeded to take the people out of the roles they were in. In this deroling process, I had the participants close their eyes and be in touch with the experiences that they had had while they were in their roles and what those experiences meant to them. Then I invited them to thank the character whom they were playing for offering him or herself to them, saying goodbye to the character and taking the name tag off. I asked them to think of their own name and to see themselves in terms of the dwelling that they would be going to that evening, to get a picture of their kitchen, their bathroom, and to stay with that until they got a full sense of themselves. I invited them to open their eyes when they were through with the process. Then I inquired if anyone wanted to share anything that they gained for themselves from the family reconstruction.

Several members related how they could understand some things about their lives and their families that they hadn't seen before, and how helpful it was to be part of the family reconstruction.

I believe that this family reconstruction had a powerful influence on Ann because she allowed herself to be so open and to feel her feelings to the depth that she did. This journey began with Ann having a one-sided picture and set of feelings for her mother and for her father. These were the simplistic perceptions of a child. After exploring her three families, Ann ended the journey understanding the complexity of her parents and seeing the various dynamics that shaped them to be the way they were. This new understanding brought Ann to a new set of feelings—for her mother in particular. The anger, hatred and coldness melted into a softness, into empathy, compassion and forgiveness. Whereas previously Ann could hardly bring herself to embrace her mother, she ended by hugging her with tears and love. It was indeed a long day's journey into light!

A final note: There were scenes and dialogues from this family reconstruction not mentioned here. I have tried to capture the highlights in these chapters. The entire work from interview to conclusion took some five to six hours.

8 THE JOURNEY'S AFTERMATH

A few final questions must be raised: Will the family reconstruction have any lasting benefit for Ann? Will it bring about any real change between And and her parents? Will it enable Ann to be more expressive about her anger and her negative feelings? Will she feel her own power and be less depressed? Will her self-esteem grow?

I believe the answers to these questions depend on several things. From my experience I would judge that Ann's learning during her family reconstruction was deep enough to have a lasting effect. But more is needed.

Ann needs to see this experience as a beginning. New pictures, new feelings, new experiences were opened for her. Now that a door is opened, she has to keep walking through and beyond it. She needs to practice and repeat the new ways. There must be a conscious effort to integrate these new ways into her life. A family reconstruction is no magical cure or instant miracle. It is a powerful beginning or a powerful strengthening of what may already have begun. It can be the starting rocket launching the spacecraft or a booster rocket fired midway in flight.

The critical need to put into practice new behavior in the days that follow the reconstruction reminds me of a friend of mine who went to a golf school last year. During each of the five days he had to hit 500 golf balls a day with an instructor watching him at all times. Any time he reverted to his old habits, the instructor corrected him. He hit 2500 balls in five days, getting blisters on his hands, as well as aching arm and shoulder muscles, simply to repeat new behavior until it became a habit. Even at that, the instructor said clearly to my friend, "If you don't go home and continue vigorous practice for the next year, you have wasted a thousand dollars in coming here!" If it takes such practice just to change a set of motions and muscle reactions in a golf swing, how much more is needed for a psychological habit?

Ann may need some help in continuing what the family reconstruction started. It doesn't have to be professional help. She may be in some sort of support group. She may have a few close friends. Many Explorers are in AA or Al-Anon. It is important for the Guide to point out that if the family reconstruction is powerful enough, the repercussions may go on for months, even years. As a Guide I check to see if the Explorer has some help available, whether professional or otherwise.

I believe Ann will relate differently to her mother due to the depth I saw in the family reconstruction experience. My guess is that as Ann approaches her mother, this new awareness and understanding will be communicated on some level. There is a chance that Mary will receive the communication and be altered by it. Certainly Mary will be affected by being understood by her daughter. If that grows then the real Mary may feel like the role-playing Mary: "For the first time I'm understood." If this occurs then the relationship will change dramatically, much like Andrea's account in the first chapter.

If this doesn't happen, all is not lost. Ann can still work on not being hooked by Mary's old intrusive ways and maintaining the understanding of her mother. From that Ann can accept her mother as she is without being overwhelmed that she hasn't changed. In so far as Ann maintains a different attitude and response to her mother, her mother has to deal with a new Ann. That dyadic system will have changed even if it looks as though Mary hasn't. But in time Mary too will shift ground if Ann can maintain her new loving, compassionate and accepting stance. Even if nothing new occurs between Ann and Mary (highly unlikely, but possible), this family reconstruction will have added to Ann's self-esteem. Prior to the family reconstruction Ann was negating her mother with anger and distance. In a very real but invisible way, then, Ann was negating part of herself, because Mary is part of Ann's root system. To negate or cut off part of oneself diminishes one's self-esteem.

The more I guide family reconstructions, the more I see that the two greatest benefits are the least seen by the Explorer. At the end of the family reconstruction, the Explorer will be aware of new pictures, insights and understandings. She will know she has gone through new experiences and has felt differently. She may even be aware of the rules of survival that have hampered growth. She will be able to tell you how helpful these new experiences will be in her life down the line. However, two other results from the family reconstruction may not seem as important to the Explorer.

The first is the fact that the Explorer has come to experience her parents more as ordinary human beings like herself than as "parents," authority figures or infallible gods who somehow control her existence. To have a total psychological experience (not a mere intellectual appreciation) of Mom and Dad as Mary and Peter is critical to the possibility of lasting changes in the Explorer. The power parents have held over the Explorer is broken or dispelled by their being reduced to the level of simple human beings like the Explorer herself.

Why do parents and their teachings, modeling and influence have such a powerful hold over their children, even when the children are 37 years old? Why are early learnings so hard to change? The reason is that a child is so vulnerable, so dependent upon these giants (parents) in order to survive, that she will do anything the parents want in order not to jeopardize their love and approval. Thus, these giants take on god-like qualities of being all-knowing, all-powerful and perfect. As long as the 37-year-old daughter still unconsciously carries this divine impression of her parents, she will find it hard to change or go against these giants in her life. In the family reconstruction, as she experiences them as human, the stranglehold is broken.

In Ann's case, Mom and Dad are now experienced as Mary and Peter—with fears, sexual drives, failings, loneliness, vulnerabilities, confusions, ignorances. Ann begins to sense, "Indeed they are human like me. They were as dependent on their parents as I. They were as stuck in changing as I am. They couldn't see their parents as humans either." On an unconscious level, she thinks, "*I am as powerful as they.* So I can change what I want!"

The second less obvious benefit of experiencing all of one's roots is equally critical. I am more and more convinced that on some profound level every person knows she or he is more than what meets the eye. A person is like a whole tree with a vast network of nourishing, life-sustaining roots hidden beneath the surface. The feelings we have about ourselves are about the *whole* self, not just that part that appears above ground. So when the family reconstruction retraces a person's formative experiences, even down to the root system that includes both sets of grandparents, that which was missing, forgotten and suppressed is brought to light. This experience of wholeness subtly and unconsciously adds to the Explorer's self-esteem.

This holds true even if some of the tree seems "defective"—such as the presence of an abuser, a criminal, a mentally ill person or an alcoholic. During the family reconstruction the Explorer is able to understand with compassion these dysfunctional or limited parts, whether in family members or in the self. Hiding or avoiding parts of one's tree damages one's self-esteem because the underlying message of avoidance is: "There must be something not okay about me.'' Accepting the entirety of one's history, including the limited, conveys and reinforces the message that being limited is okay; it is part of the human condition. So when the Explorer uncovers all of his roots as an adult, the appreciation of his fullness and self-worth grows on a deep, unconscious level. No wonder the TV series ''Roots'' was so appealing to millions of viewers. So convinced am I of these two benefits that if the Explorer receives no new great ''ahas'' during a family reconstruction, experiencing one's parents as humans and one's roots as alive will make the family reconstruction a rewarding day's journey.

About five months after Ann's family reconstruction, I received a letter from her in which she described her life's journey since the reconstruction. I quote from her letter:

''Since the family reconstruction there have been some subtle changes in how I think about my mother. I'm not sure our outward relating to each other has changed much—I don't see my parents more than a few times a month, although I talk on the phone with my dad frequently. I see my mother with more depth and her personal history more than I'd previously contemplated. I feel more compassionate and tolerant toward her, although still not willing to free her from accountability for her failure to deal more positively with the crucial issues in her life that impacted on the rest of my family. Also I feel more differentiated from her. It sounds so trite when put into words; I feel I'm quoting from a Psych I textbook: 'I feel more separate, like I have a separate identity and we *are* really different people, and she can be mean and crazy and anything else and that doesn't mean I'll be like that ''when I grow up.''' You get the picture.

''For me, generally, my job has changed dramatically—I have been increasingly busy, learning a lot and loving it all. My social life has also been quite active. I often come to work Monday tired from all the activities of the weekend! By Wednesday I've recovered enough to start planning for the weekend to come. I've even been going out with men! I've lost about 15 pounds and started wearing makeup, which I haven't done for about seven years—i.e., I'm having fun. I'm currently learning a form of Tai Chi. So things are pretty positive and flowing, I'd say.''

9 THE DAY'S JOURNEY ENLIGHTENS ALL FAMILIES

Ann's family, while unique, is similar to all families. The human needs and dynamics operating in her family are the same for any family. The central theme of this book, as well as of Ann's life and of all family systems, is self-worth.

Self-worth or esteem is that basic attitude and feeling we carry around about ourselves. Our self-worth is high or low depending upon what our attitude is regarding ourselves. Since so many other things are connected to self-worth, it is safe to say that our highest achievement is to arrive at a point in life where we enjoy high self-esteem on a sustained basis. This does not mean that our self-worth is never bruised. From a state of high self-worth, self-confidence, high energy, creativity and a host of other positive realities flow. This state of being is brought about by many elements operating in some sort of simultaneity.

The attitude of high self-worth is one that is able to respect, honor, cherish and accept oneself entirely and unconditionally, including one's limitations, failures and resulting scars. Any attitude that disrespects or ignores or condemns or is unaccepting of any part of oneself (such as one's failures) leads to low self-esteem. Usually a person with this attitude will not even honor her ''good'' parts. We all know the feelings associated with high or low self-esteem. Thus, the great developmental quest in life is to achieve high self-esteem. In order to do this one must know the ingredients of self-esteem and how they go together.

High self-worth involves honoring and accepting all that makes up oneself. From my experience there are certain key elements of the person that are typically not respected or accepted. One element of the human being that is frequently overlooked, denied, ignored or rejected is one's entire family system. A person tends to think of her reality as that being circumscribed by her skin. Yet a person is part of a family tree system, the most vital parts of which go back three generations. How often will a part of a family be unknown or deliberately shunned? The family drunk or institutionalized person can never be talked about, as if that part of the system doesn't even exist. The message is clear: "Do not accept that part of you."

Another reality that is often discounted is the paradox of being completely unique yet somehow the same as all other persons. Often people are as afraid to express themselves as adults as they were as children in a classroom, fearing to ask a question—because they think they were the only ones with misunderstandings or puzzles. Yet everyone has puzzles. In this respect each of us is like every other person in the world. Such behavior implies the message: "It is not human to have puzzles and misunderstandings."

It is also not unusual to see people raised to be so like mother or father that they do not feel their own feelings, they do not reach out for what they want; they fail to experience their own uniqueness. They so deny their individuality that they never develop their own differences and uniqueness. The message they have received is: "Don't be yourself."

A third key element of the human person that is often dishonored and rejected is one's "negative" parts, such as limitations, weaknesses, failures, mistakes, sins. When those parts are not accepted, then one-half of the person is cut off, denied. One's full reality is not honored; only the "positive" aspects are accepted. The message is: "Being human allows no negatives."

A fourth element I find frequently ignored is the human need to have three modalities of life: to be alone, to be intimate with one other, and to be involved in society. Many people stay to themselves in their innermost being, never sharing the depth of their feelings and thoughts with anyone. They can't trust others—or can't trust themselves to cope adequately with betrayal or hurt if it should occur in human life. Or they believe they are not worthy enough for anyone to be interested in the depth of their reality. On the other hand, I often see people who feel so needy of other people that they spend their lives clinging and being with others. They can't stand to be alone. Then there are others afraid to venture out into society. Each such venture is filled with stress for them. The messages behind all this are: "You can't trust people." "You are not worthy of intimacy." "You are not sufficient enough or worthy enough to be alone and enjoy yourself." "You will never make it in the world." All of this in some way dishonors and fails to accept that part of oneself that needs a balance among those three ways of living.

These are four realities of personhood I find most frequently disrespected and not accepted. When a person so dishonors herself or parts of herself she is putting herself down; this attitude leads to feelings of low self-esteem. When these central realities are respected, then the full person is accepted and esteemed with high value.

So the ingredients making up high self-esteem are all those aspects that go together to make up the complete human personality. All of one's reality must be seen, valued and accepted.

Because high self-esteem is so critical to personal well being, it is worth studying the forces that lead people to honor or dishonor, accept or reject some or all parts of their personality. The scheme at the end of this chapter attempts to diagram the elements that influence this process. Some people are raised to relate congruently, i.e., to express in clear and honest ways what we are really thinking and feeling. Others are not raised in this way. Some are raised with rules that forbid them to respect, accept and deal with all of human reality. Others' rules permit this openness. Some are raised with a set of meanings, a value system, and a philosophy of life that honors failures and weaknesses. Others must despise such weakness. Some are raised to cope with threats in ways that allow them to deal with the situation as a whole. Others learn to cut off parts of reality (e.g., blamers cut off the other person, placators deny their own needs). Whenever we are raised to avoid, deny or distort any of our reality we are given the hidden message: "There is something wrong with you."

Having summarized the basic theme of this book we can now look at Ann's family reconstruction within this framework to see how Ann's self-esteem was affected by her family experience and what took place during the family reconstruction to enhance it.

Ann's desire to heal the relationship with a mother who encroached upon and threatened her means that somehow Ann experienced her mother as a powerful figure who said, in effect, "Don't be yourself" and "There are unacceptable parts of you." The issue, then, is the continuing damage to Ann's self-esteem because of the messages she continues to receive about restraining the full expression of her full personhood.

The fact that she left out the chronology of her mother's and father's families indicates how she cuts off her family system, in some way viewing them as not important. Again she is denying part of herself. Not being able to fantasize her mother's birth is another way of cutting off her mother, a crucial part of her. Ann's attitude that there is something wrong with her is apparent when she shows that some parts of her and her family are not to be fully owned and accepted.

In the interview I stressed how her mother had learned from her upbringing to be the way she was. Stressing this was important, as Ann unconsciously felt that her mother was "just that way"—either from her genetic package or by conscious deliberation. If we are totally fixed by our genes, there is no hope. If we are totally the way we are by full deliberation, there is hardly any room for compassion. However, if our being is explained in the more complicated yet real way—as a combination of genes, free will and powerful early rearing—then there is room for compassion and acceptance. Leaving out her mother's history was an easy way for Ann to continue to believe the worst about her mother, as she had all her life. However, through the family reconstruction Ann was able to see how her mother came to be the way she was through a set of unique, subtle and complicated dynamics. So at the end of the day's journey, Ann could see her mother realistically (respect), appreciate her struggles and strengths (honor), be compassionate toward her weaknesses (cherish) and finally engage her mother in a loving embrace as a human being called Mary (accept). In accepting Mary, Ann was accepting herself, as Mary is a powerful part of her.

When Ann keeps hidden her painful and angry feelings, she is acting as if they are unacceptable feelings. She had learned a rule from her father Peter: "Don't be angry." With this rule she learned to dishonor her angry part, to not accept it. Here was another piece of her that was unacceptable. The result was low self-esteem. Furthermore, by not using her anger she failed to experience power. Being impotent in the face of threat undermines self-esteem. Ann admitted that she walked through life not feeling sure about what was going to happen to her.

As we reconstructed Peter's family, Ann discovered to her amazement how her father Peter learned from his father Larry to keep Ann helpless so that Peter would feel important about himself. As long as Ann is helpless, Peter has an important function to play in the family—taking care of helpless Ann. By not using her anger, Ann certainly could stay helpless! Ann also saw how Peter's father, her Grampa McConnell, treated her the same way. Ann's eyes were now opening to see some limitations of her father, whom she idolized. As she allowed herself to accept her father with some weaknesses, she would be open to doing the same for her mother. When Ann could accept the weaknesses and failures of her parts—mother and father—then she could more easily accept the limitations within herself.

As Peter felt trapped, protected and controlled by June, he began to question, doubt and disown his own uniqueness. This prepared him to enter into a marriage with low self-esteem, unless between childhood and marriage he could learn how to honor his total self. Apparently he hadn't because he admitted to Ann that he married a woman as controlling as his mother. It was as if Peter needed a woman to continue to protect him by exerting complete control.

Ann also saw how her father was not in touch with his anger toward his father, Larry. Again she saw how weak he was with both parents. Ann's eyes were opening to the limitations of her father. He was becoming as human as Ann! She even could feel some anger in herself toward him for not protecting her from her mother.

When we reconstructed Ann's mother's family, Ann could see her mother Mary in an entirely new light. Ann saw how Mary was raised to be so right she could never be her unique self, honoring her own particular needs and wants. Ann now understood Mary and felt compassion toward her. Ann was seeing Mary as a human being. She accepted Mary and, in so doing, accepted an important part of herself—leading to a higher self-esteem.

As we began Ann's family of origin on Sunday, Ann reported that in some way the experience on Saturday had enabled her to see an important rule in her family: "Never show negative feelings" or "Always be happy." Obviously, such a rule prohibiting any unhappy feelings makes a person disrespect and dishonor those feelings that are part and parcel of everyone's existence. So again, Ann is reared so as not to be accepting of herself fully—resulting in low self-worth.

As related in Chapter 7, Peter and Mary were able to share how they both could have transmitted that rule to her. I seized the moment to let Ann see that she was like her mother—unable to express both negative and unhappy feelings. Ann grew closer to appreciating and accepting her mother.

Then, at that very moment, Ann was able to report that she didn't feel good the night before when all the others in the group reported feeling very positively! Within the process of the family reconstruction, Ann was breaking her rule about not sharing unhappy feelings. I honored this immediately—contrary to what her parents had done to her in the past. I repeat an earlier observation: If a person covers up a feeling, the embedded message is that feeling must not be okay: "There must be something wrong with me."

I am now going to stop my analysis of the family reconstruction and challenge you to continue on your own. Reread Chapter 7 and look at Ann's family reconstruction within the framework presented. In this way you will begin to look at a family in terms of self-worth and in terms of the dynamics that set up the rules, meanings and coping mechanisms that lead a person to accept or not accept all of oneself. As you do this you will be preparing yourself to engage in the exercises described in the Appendix designed to help you unlock the family within you.

Notice in Ann's family the lines of communication; detect the rules of survival; try to decipher embedded meanings. As you become more skilled in understanding how these dynamics influence Ann's self-worth, you will become more skilled in understanding the evolution of your own self-esteem. How did important people relate to you when you were growing up? What meanings were you taught about life experiences? What rules were you taught? What things

Figure 21. The growth of self esteem

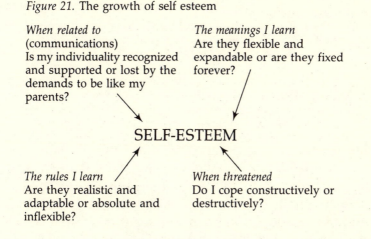

When related to
(communications)
Is my individuality recognized
and supported or lost by the
demands to be like my
parents?

The meanings I learn
Are they flexible and
expandable or are they fixed
forever?

SELF-ESTEEM

The rules I learn
Are they realistic and
adaptable or absolute and
inflexible?

When threatened
Do I cope constructively or
destructively?

threatened you or made you uneasy? How did you handle being threatened? How did these four elements help you to honor and accept or to dishonor and reject parts of your self? All this bears on how well or how badly you think and feel about yourself.

Figure 21 summarizes the process whereby a person, especially a child, gathers a sense of his or her self-esteem. The process of the development of self-esteem begins at birth when the child absorbs the family's behavior, some of which is dysfunctional. The process continues through childhood and adolescence into adulthood. We arrive at positive self-esteem if we challenge the dysfunctional parts of our rearing and make modifications to fit our unique personality. If we do not challenge the dysfunctional parts of the process, we block off and dishonor parts of ourselves and reality, and our self-esteem fails to grow.

10 A GUIDE'S COMPASS AND MAP

As I prepare for a family reconstruction, the first thing I reflect on is how this will be an adventure for me. I ponder how this family is different from any family I have ever encountered. I do not know much about this family at this stage, even though I have some guesses based on my knowledge of the Explorer and the homework submitted to me. All my guesses are held as mere possibilities. I do not want to get too attached to any preconceived notion of what might be going on within this person and the families involved. My hunches are only doors I will open to see what is really there.

I am guided by the dilemma the Explorer has described and wants to work on. For example, Chris wanted to become more assertive, especially with women. As I looked over his family reconstruction homework, I searched for clues to how he learned submission and what the payoffs might be for being submissive. However, I remain tentative enough in my initial analysis to be ready to shift to another, possibly deeper dilemma that neither the Explorer nor I am aware of as we begin the day's journey. When we got into Chris's family reconstruction, what became apparent was how much of his energy was still tied to his grandmother, who had died when he was 10 years old. It was important to release that energy for his use by allowing him and encouraging him to grieve his loss, cry, and say goodbye to his beloved grandmother.

Each family reconstruction is an exciting mystery. I am

a detective trying to unravel the hidden dynamics of the three families so that I and the Explorer—as well as the group—can solve the mystery together. Most of the time we do, and the final scene is reminiscent of the old *Thin Man* or *Charlie Chan* movies where all the pieces tie together to everyone's great astonishment and delight.

Since this is a team effort, I stay close to the Explorer during the day—to be in his or her energy field and to pick up the vibes, the palpitations, the slightest movements hidden to the less observant person. From these I get cues as to whether we are on the right track, and as to what is significant. For example, when I note a sudden rush of feelings I take the opportunity to nurture and channel those feelings in such a way that the Explorer may have an important experience at that moment. Being close to the Explorer lets me seize the right moment to gently guide what might be the breakthrough experience of the day.

All this being so, I try to prepare myself the night before so that from the moment I awake I can be alive, alert, and as observant as possible. Before the group members arrive, I try to allow time to center myself and focus on what is before me. I usually find that even if, after all my efforts, I am scattered or sluggish, the actual getting started wakes me up and the intrigue of it all sharpens my senses. Getting close to the Explorer in a trusting, caring, listening and responsive way in the opening dialogue gets me thoroughly in the here and now with full energy. I am aware of a relaxed tension in which I feel free to move like a deer.

If I still find myself distracted in some way, I either muster up greater discipline and energy to be in the here and now, or I try to figure out what is distracting me and deal with it. During one family reconstruction I found myself distracted and suddenly realized what was causing the diffusion of my energy: I had just returned to my home in Oklahoma after some months away. In my absence the housesitter had rearranged my furniture. In addition, I had recently opened a home in California and did not yet feel fully at home there. So I was somewhat dislocated in California, and now I was feeling the same in Oklahoma due to all the furniture being moved around. Unconsciously this gave me a disconnected, rootless feeling, and my energies were tied up in coping with it. I told the group, which responded sympathetically; members had noticed something was wrong and were glad I shared with them my personal discomfort. The distraction left me.

As the group assembles and members get acquainted or reacquainted with each other over coffee, I usually feel a bit shy and awkward, as do many, if not all, of the members. I am happy not to be so self-assured—it keeps me one with the group. This reminds me every time of the need to help the group begin to relax and become comfortable. I always have some exercise or device in my head that will help each member feel included. If there are more newcomers than usual, I will spend more time with the inclusion process.

After the interview with the Explorer, which I have described in Chapter 4, I am guided throughout the day by the following basic principles.

1) Family reconstruction is a process. I realize that I am guiding a process, not a person. I control the step-by-step procedure rather than the Explorer. It is within the river banks of the flowing process that the Explorer is stimulated to have his or her own actions and reactions, just as a fish carries on its own life within the flowing waters of the river. The process, not the person, depends on me.

One of the artistic subtleties that emerges from this is that I must not let myself get in the way of the process. I must not go into the family reconstruction with a preconceived notion of precisely which scenes to set up or which specific dynamics to instigate, or I could almost unconsciously manipulate the Explorer to act out my preconceived game plan.

I do not want all to applaud the results only to realize later on that the real target was missed, so it is important that I not be too attached to my guesses, hunches, and speculations as to what the issues and dynamics might be. I must be willing to shift gears quickly. Therefore, I try not to spend too much time figuring out from the homework and the interviews which issues may be at stake. I trust the unfolding process as the Explorer picks the role players, sculpts the families, and reveals personal dilemmas. I am so convinced of the accuracy of the process that I know if it is cared for properly the real issues and dynamics will emerge.

A sign to me that the process has been honored is the way the family reconstruction ends. The players are deroled and some expressions are exchanged in the group as to what various members gained for themselves. Then the group begins to disperse. When the Explorer and other members gather in twos and threes, exchanging intimate thanks and good wishes, if I remain just one of the members, then I know the whole process has worked. If, on the other hand, I become the center of attention after the people begin to disperse, then that is a sign to me that I have played too prominent a role. The goal of the entire family reconstruction is to empower the Explorer and the people in the group. I am a servant to that happening. If that empowerment has taken place, the Explorer is the natural center of energy, the magnet drawing energy and concern from the other participants.

2) Remove the veil. I want to help all group members—the Explorer, the alter ego and the role players—to be aware of their deepest and most hidden thoughts and feelings, to lift up what has not been seen or felt before. So I am constantly asking the people to close their eyes and be aware of all going on inside of them, and then to report that to the group. Unveiling hidden feelings and thoughts is critical if the Explorer is to experience new things.

3) Get the Explorer to act in a new way. I constantly look for opportunities to get the Explorer into the action, especially when I see the Explorer particularly moved by what is transpiring. I will, for example, encourage the Explorer to go up and tell his uncle what he is thinking or feeling; or ask the alter ego to speak directly to the Explorer and have the Explorer respond; or have the Explorer assume the same sculpted position as he has just created for his alter ego. I look for every opportunity to have the Explorer enter into a new experience.

When the Explorer is given to intellectualizing everything, or resisting emotional involvement because it is too threatening, I look for every possible way to involve him or her. A good example of this is seen in Chapter 6 when I asked Ann to play the parts of each member of her mother's family. Up to that point Ann was keeping herself from getting emotionally connected with the scene and with her mother. As she played each member of the family she became emotionally engaged and deeply affected by what was happening to her mother in that family.

The dilemma the Explorer is working on guides me in choosing which new experiences to emphasize. If the Explorer is working on how to be more expressive with anger, for example, then when I see anger begin to emerge I will encourage him to express it—a new experience. If the Explorer never showed anger (for example, to his mother) and he does so during the family reconstruction, the new experience could be quite freeing, especially when he sees that the strong feelings destroyed neither the mother nor the self. A new experience that contains a great deal of affect will be more powerful than a mere new intellectual insight.

4) Fill in the missing parts. If the Explorer is very well acquainted with mother's family and hardly knows father's family, I will usually develop father's family first and spend more time on that rather than focusing on what is already known. What is at stake here is the need for each person to be whole. When the Explorer's father's side of the family is such a blank, a huge piece is missing from that person's whole family. While this may sound simplistic, my experience of its profound truth is so strong that I am satisfied that enormous help is given to an Explorer if nothing happens in the family reconstruction other than filling out the entire family picture. The completed picture in some mysterious way lets the Explorer feel more at peace, more confident and strong as an individual, more whole. When a significant part of our root system is missing, we go through life maimed in a sense. Even if the missing pieces are disfigured and negative, their discovery still completes the whole!

5) *Add missing psychological states.* If a person views his life as all drab and dull, I try to add many scenes of laughter, lightness and gaiety. If a person sees himself as only bad, I try to add some positive aspects; likewise, I try to add some negative aspects if the perceptions are all rosy. It is important for the Explorer to see the members of his family as real human beings rather than as stereotypes, be they devils or saints. I suspect there is hardly any human being who is totally serious or totally lighthearted, or all stupid or all brilliant. The Explorer needs to see the vulnerability in the strong and the strength in the weak.

6) *Life is complex.* I try to help the Explorer see the complexities of the human personality and of the human situation. As we grow up we are simply incapable of understanding these complexities. Thus we develop simplistic perceptions with attendant powerful feelings and attitudes. Helping the Explorer become liberated means shattering these lifelong early childhood perceptions. Letting the Explorer experience the mother and father and their life situations as complex helps the Explorer humanize the parents. These newly gained perceptions can then begin to alter the feelings within the Explorer.

7) Include external influences. It is sometimes valuable to take into account an outside system that affected the families being developed in the family reconstruction. Once during the family reconstruction of a person who came from a Mormon background, I sculpted a person up on a chair with a Bible in his hand and a pointing finger saying, "Always do God's will." Once the impact of church authority was added, the whole scene was charged with electricity and things began to make sense.

Another time I was guiding the family reconstruction of a black woman who felt abandoned by her father. She had come to almost hate him; certainly she did not trust him. She had very strong feelings about not having babies since her own childhood had been so terrible (as she had been told by her mother); her father neglected the family and drank too much. She had little information about and few inner pictures of her father's family. The family reconstruction homework told me that her father's and mother's families had lived within five miles of each other. In doing her family reconstruction, I made sure all those extended members were sculpted, even in scenes involving only two or three people. I wanted her to see how truly surrounded she was—especially by her father's family, with whom the mother and father lived for the first four years of their marriage! Until her family reconstruction, this fact had been overlooked by the Explorer. In seeing this, she began to see that indeed her father's family was not the total washout that her mother had led her to believe.

The example of the Mormon shows the influence of an external system upon the family. The example of the black woman shows the influence of the extended family. The point of this seventh principle is that any external system that may have a bearing on a single person or on a nuclear family needs to be brought in so that the Explorer can see how he and the nuclear family are affected by the larger system. Some powerful external systems that often affect family life and therefore play important functions in the family reconstruction are the Depression of the 1930s, the persecution of the Jews in Europe, the two World Wars, the role of the Church, and the mobility of society.

8) Communicate directly. I seize every opportunity during the family reconstruction to have the role players correct skewed communication patterns. If I spot members of the family giving double messages or withholding parts of their true feelings, I will let that scene unfold and then I will redo the scene, inviting the role players to be in touch with everything they are feeling and to communicate that straightforwardly. This allows the Explorer to see and experience that honest and free communication within the family might have led to quite a different outcome. This is a powerful lesson. To facilitate this, I usually ask a role player to close his or her eyes, see what is going on within, become conscious of thoughts and feeling, especially those that have not been expressed. Then I invite the role player to express that which has been left unexpressed. Another way to do this is to ask all the role players to be aware of what they are wanting at the present moment, and then to go after it.

9) Overcome resistance. During a family reconstruction, I constantly watch for resistance because this indicates possible areas of significant blockage for the Explorer. At each of these points of resistance, I firmly but gently challenge the Explorer to walk through the resistance. Yet I am respectful of the resistance. If the Explorer adamantly refuses, then I know it is important to keep this resistance for now. He or she is not ready yet. All does not need to be done in a single family reconstruction! If the Explorer balks, I will at least deal with that phenomenon by asking what he or she is afraid of and by saying that it is all right to maintain those feelings. I just want the Explorer to be aware of the resistance and how it may or may not be useful.

Many times an Explorer will not accept the new picture of mother or father unfolding in the scene being acted out. Or the Explorer will not be willing to reveal thoughts and feelings to mother or father. In such a case I ask the Explorer: "Can you at least be open to this as a possibility? Will you speak to your father step by step, trying on each statement one at a time? Remember, it's safe. These are not your real parents. It doesn't mean you will ever have to do this in real life—there may be no need to if we can do it now!"

10) *Everyone has something to contribute.* All members of the group, especially those playing the roles, have a piece to add to the entire picture unfolding. Therefore, I almost always ask each role player what he or she is experiencing in the scene. It is not sufficient to only get reactions from the Explorer and the alter ego.

11) *Avoid multiplicity of scenes and experiences.* I prefer that the Explorer deeply perceive and experience a few items rather than a plethora of ideas, insights and experiences that are more superficially grasped. Thus I stay with a scene that is arousing a great deal of reaction rather than rush on to complete more scenes. It is important to be very observant to catch the flickers of reaction. Sometimes they surface and then are quickly suppressed as they are threatening in some way. I also prefer to stop when the Explorer is feeling exhausted. Many times the Explorer will say, "I can't experience another thing." A family reconstruction can be a very draining experience. Again, not all needs to be done in one day. Again if I see in the opening minutes of the family reconstruction, perhaps in the very choosing of the role players, that the Explorer is emotionally moved, I will invite the Explorer to stay with the feeling and let it grow. After a few moments I suggest that the Explorer speak directly to the characters. Sometimes the real breakthrough of a family reconstruction will occur within the first hour,

with the rest of the action confirming what has already been achieved.

12) Search for the meaning behind incongruous happenings. If the Explorer has described the grandmother as strong, angry and domineering, and then chooses a person from the group who is mild, soft and placating, then that is incongruous. Incongruities can be a particular form of resistance and therefore should be dealt with. Resistances are points of major breakthroughs.

I once failed to catch such an incongruity. The Explorer, Terese, picked a mild man to play the part of a strong, expressive and angry grandfather who supposedly greatly influenced his son, Terese's father. Due to this incongruity, the person playing her father was not properly enrolled. He didn't feel the impact of a strong, angry father as he grew up. Thus, while Terese's real father was terrified by anger, the role playing father was not prepared for that role. This warped the reconstruction until I finally realized what was wrong. I had to intervene to change the role player. Then I had Terese deal with what I had done. This interchange made evident why she had chosen so incongruently. She was protecting herself from dealing with her scared father. So she picked a grandfather who would not raise a terrified son.

13) Use myself fully. I try to stay constantly in touch with what I am feeling, thinking and picturing; what I feel like doing; what puzzles me. Even if I get a crazy idea out of nowhere—with no inkling of how it is connected to anything but just a feeling of excitement about it—then I'll say this to the people and say that I would like to experiment with it. If I detect some fear in me, I respect and deal with it, try to figure out if it is due to my own past history or if it is emanating from what is occurring in the family reconstruction. In the end, I am the best compass of what is going on and where we are in the process. I trust myself more than anything or anyone else.

I question my own reactions only when I am disturbed about something in my personal life. That kind of stress diminishes my faculties and tends to make me subjective, out of contact with what is happening outside myself. When I am under personal stress I tend to respond to my own internal state rather than to the external process of the family reconstruction. If I am fairly content within myself, then I can be in touch with what is going on externally and be responsive to it.

These are the 13 principles that guide me as I do a family reconstruction. Seldom am I consciously aware of the functioning of these principles. Their implementation is as automatic and second nature to me as riding a bicycle or swinging a golf club. I am sure that other principles operate at times that I am not able to identify. However, these 13 are the pivotal ones to me in guiding a family reconstruction.

11 THE EXPLORER ENCOUNTERS TWO BASIC PARADOXES

In order to grow and achieve the heights of human experience, in order to enter into the spiritual and mystical levels of human existence, a person must constantly deal with realities best described as paradoxes—apparent contradictions. Of all these paradoxes I believe that there are two that are most basic to human development. One is expressed by "He who seeks his life will lose it and he who loses his life will find it." The other is expressed by "Love your enemies." Family reconstruction is a day's journey during which both of these paradoxes are encountered and experienced.

Sometimes in therapy and in the human potential movement you hear the admonitions: "You can be the master of your own destiny." "You can be in charge of yourself." "You are in charge of what you want to be, of who you want to be, of what you want from life." The legitimacy of such banner statements stems from the fact that so many people are submissive, passive, powerless, helpless, overly dependent in such a way that they have never developed their own personhood. These people have never established their own individual boundaries. As such they are depressed and feel badly about themselves. With such low self-esteem they achieve little in life compared to what they could. As a result they deprive the rest of humanity of the gifts they could offer, so everyone loses.

To counteract this phenomenon, therapists often encourage people to achieve control of their own lives, to be in charge of themselves, to be less dependent. Such an endeavor is admirable; however, it can be both advocated and construed to mean, "You will be totally in charge of yourself and your destiny." This can easily lead to the embedded message, "You can do it alone." A variation of this embedded message is, "Don't trust others, trust only yourself." This self-sufficiency and independence may lead to estrangement. Such isolation cuts one off from participating in the loving energy present in other people, the universe, and what many refer to as God. Paradoxically this leads one to be out of control, powerless, since one is cut off from the loving power of others. A certain trusting in or surrendering to others is needed.

This apparent contradiction (to control oneself versus to surrender control) is captured in the statement, "He who seeks his life will lose it, he who loses his life will find it." The following story describes the phenomenon.

Several years ago I spent a couple of weeks with Brugh Joy, M.D., in the desert of central California. We were meditating, fasting, and trying other methods of moving into an altered state of consciousness. During the three-day fasting period, I decided to take a long hike into the desert, which was bristling with sharp cactus. I was in shorts and tennis shoes. At first I tried to be in control and guide myself in stepping here and there to avoid being scratched by the cactus and desert growth. I was not too successful.

Then I decided to surrender to my feet and to the desert, and to stop trying to use my head to be in control. I decided to trust the desert to pull my feet in whichever direction it wanted. I was on top of a large, high hill. I defocused my eyes (helped by my contact lenses being out, leaving me with 20-200 vision in the left eye and 20-40 in the right eye) and began my descent. I picked up speed and fell into a rhythmic running. I soon found myself dancing through the desert growth, swaying one way and then another, being one with the immediate space in front of me, not looking ahead to be in control. I experienced trusting something beyond me, something outside of my own control. I felt a surrendering, a oneness and connection I hadn't felt when I was trying to control myself to protect my legs from being scratched. I felt out of control while at the same time in perfect control. Needless to say, after the long descent I had not scratched myself once! In losing my life, I found it. When I had sought my life earlier I was losing it.

When people misconstrue the message "You can be in charge of your own life" as meaning "You alone can be in control of your destiny," they can become subtly egotistical. The "I can" and "I am" become the center of their life's pursuits. I think there is a parallel to this in some people who are into the "health" movement. They preoccupy themselves with researching every health food, vitamin, and latest bodily improvement method with such a compulsion that I often wonder if the terror of dying is not deeply buried behind all this activity. What is their capacity to surrender to death? Being free and open to dying might so relax a person that he or she becomes truly healthy. Being driven to achieve health may so stress a person that she or he becomes sick.

As I see it, one of the tasks of life is to learn in some way to give up control—in order to achieve it! This experience of giving up control in such a way that one gains control is found in the process of the family reconstruction itself. In a successful family reconstruction, the Explorer surrenders to the process, not knowing what explains it all, not knowing what is ahead in the day's journey, not knowing what the outcome will be. And being in such ignorance the Explorer usually moves through fear and anxiety at the beginning of the day to a growing peaceful trust in the Guide, the group and the process. As the giving up of oneself in trust grows throughout the day, the paradoxical result begins to develop—the Explorer begins in some diffused, inchoate way to discover himself or herself being more together, in control, confident and powerful. The Explorer's limited perceptions are shattered, the feelings attached to those perceptions disappear, more complete perceptions and feelings begin to take their place, and a new self-identity begins to emerge. A new way to see self, others and the world begins growing.

This awkward newness often takes months to finally blossom into a feeling of an integrated wholeness. Often at the end of the one day's journey, the Explorer can feel rather jumbled inside, as if a lot of furniture has been moved around without being finally rearranged. The redecoration of the interior house is still in process. Trying a piece here and a piece there, seeing how it fits, rearranging again until a harmonious and integrated whole is achieved may take months. A successful family reconstruction, then, is one that initiates a process of trusting in something beyond oneself, that leads to a reordering or reconstruction of oneself.

This is best achieved when the family reconstruction is led by a Guide who has no vested interest in controlling the Explorer or in making the Explorer dependent on him or her. The Guide sees clearly that she or he is in charge of the process and not the person, and sees that empowerment is one of the central tasks. I have heard Virginia Satir say over and over that we are in charge of the process—*not* the person. With such a Guide the Explorer will experience a surrendering that leads to being in control.

Each time a person has such a paradoxical experience the door is open for the person to continue having other such experiences, so that one's life can be an accumulated experience of losing oneself to find oneself. The door is open to trust that which is beyond oneself, to risk entering into those experiences that have been described repeatedly in religious literature as being one with God, Buddha, the cosmos, the universal loving energy.

Placing oneself into the hands of a higher realm is described by thousands of people as the breakthrough to peace, harmony and oneness—a feeling of being in control, empowered. This is no easy task; pain and struggle are often involved, and it is always being achieved. Sages of all cultures have warned in their writings against surrendering to an evil or harmful presence. To me a sign of that is simply whether the person becomes more dependent, less defined, less individualized rather than truly in control. The people of Jonestown exemplify the case of surrender to another so as to become more controlled and dependent. Anti-Nazi theologian, Martin Niemöller, Gandhi and Jesus exemplify the case of surrendering to another to become more in personal control, to become more individualized and independent, to lead courageous lives facing the pain involved in confronting conventional wisdom.

The second paradox is embedded in the apparently strange, illogical and impractical comment, "Love your enemies, do good to those who hate you." A variation of this message, which I think is a prerequisite before we can love our enemies, is "Love the enemy inside you, do good to that which afflicts you 'from within.'" How can we love our neighbor, nay even our enemies, if we can't love ourselves, nay even the enemy within ourselves?

All growth movements have as a basic message, "You should change." In religion the specific message is "You should change from being a sinner into being a saint." In education it is "Don't be ignorant, be smart." In all forms of therapy the message is "Get well." The message of the humanistic movement is, of course, "Be more human."

Under the message "You should change" could be a deeper message: "You ought not be the way you are" or "You are not okay the way you are." If this is so, then the various growth movements could be suggesting some degree of self-rejection, self-contempt and self-hatred.

When the emphasis on growth is put into a future goal to be reached (for example, "I'm going to get rid of this depression," "I'm going to be sinless," "I'm going to walk

again''), and when that future is strongly desired or pos-
sessed, then there is the possibility of a profound embedded message: ''I'm not okay as I am. In this present moment I don't like myself, I can't stand myself. I will only like
myself when I'm no longer depressed, no longer sinful, or
can walk again.'' This embedded message will be present
the more people concentrate on applying energies, skills,
techniques, methodologies and theories to change, rather
than on concentrating on accepting and loving themselves
presently and unconditionally.

If people flit around from one seminar to another, one
therapist or therapy to another, one religious program to the
next, and do not seem to be improving or achieving any
future change, then very possibly they could be operating
on this hidden message: ''There is something wrong with
me. I don't like myself.'' Sometimes I think that as a therapist I unwittingly buy into this hidden message and support it to the detriment of myself and my client. When I say,
''Sure, I'll help you change, I'll help you be what you
aren't,'' I may indeed be reinforcing ''You are not okay as
you are.'' Perhaps I should say to a person with such a
possible hidden self-contempt, ''No, I'm not going to help
you change. I like you as you are. I accept you with those
flaws.''

I believe this is the second most important and profound
paradox of life—and it is intimately related to the first. He
who likes himself as is will change; he who condemns himself will not change. He who strives to change will never
change; he who surrenders the struggle to change will
change. It is as if once I let go of the drivenness and anxiety that I must change, a mysterious dynamic is released that
brings about change.

Why does this paradox work? Why do I change when I
give up trying to change? I do not know all the answers to
this, but I do have two glimpses of what may be happening.

First, living organisms need the warmth of love to grow.

Hatred puts an end to living; it condemns an organism, as if something is terribly wrong with it. Self-hatred says that I must destroy myself first before I can live. Only self-love allows a person to cherish oneself as a seed developing from a limited to a more complete flowering.

Second, we tie up enormous energy in self-contempt and in living in a future that *has* to be different. Sometimes the energy tied up in self-hatred is so enormous that a person is practically paralyzed to the point that growth and movement cease. When we love ourselves as we are in the present we allow our energies to be flowing in the here and now, and thus move from moment to moment in growth.

Family reconstruction is a wonderful way to convey a self-accepting attitude. In almost every family reconstruction I have guided, a basic story line begins to emerge. The Explorer in one way or another wants mother or father to change—to be more approving, accepting or understanding, to be more loving, to stop some behavior or be somehow different. The task of the Guide is to help the Explorer give up demanding change in his parents or at least give up the kind of demanding that is associated with the hidden message, ''Change or else I'll not be happy.''

A person whose contentment and self-esteem depend on others' changing is doomed to anxiety and low self-esteem; peace will forever elude him. When the family reconstruction moves along in such a way that the Explorer finally can accept his mother and father with some understanding and compassion, even with some lingering disappointment or anger, then a great release has occurred.

A marvelous thing happens in the process of family reconstruction when the Explorer finally accepts his or her parents. The role-playing parents immediately change, drop their defenses, and open up to the Explorer. The Explorer discovers that in the very act of dropping the demand to change the parent changes! In loving the ''enemy,'' the enemy changes to a friend.

On some occasions the outcome is not so happy. Sometimes the parents are so encased in their old way of being
that they cannot change in response to the Explorer's new
acceptance and compassion—the ultimate limitation! This
challenges the Explorer to be accepting of the "enemy" even
when the enemy remains the enemy. Then the Explorer
discovers he may need to protect himself from the enemy
while accepting the enemy. However, the capacity to accept
the inimical parents leads the Explorer to protect himself
without destroying or threatening the parents and demanding that the parents change. This is the ultimate acceptance.

When this moment arrives in a family reconstruction, the
Explorer feels relief, peace and wholeness. The door is now
opened for the Explorer to accept himself. Just as the Explorer accepts his parents, so now he can accept himself with
all of his strengths and limitations. It is as if the demand on
the Explorer's part for the parents to change is a projection
of one's internal demand on oneself to change. And finally, while accepting his parents the Explorer is accepting a
large part of himself, as one's parents are part of oneself!

This is what happened to Ann in Chapter 7. She started
the day's journey not accepting her mother, yet realizing
something needed to be changed. As the day unfolded we
saw Ann trying to get her mother to understand, accept and
approve of her. In the end Ann abandoned that effort and
instead accepted her mother. After this acceptance, changes
began to flow within Ann even though it appeared that
Ann's mother had not changed.

How does a person come to be either accepting or nonaccepting of oneself? If a child is related to in an accepting
way by one's parents, then the child learns how to accept
oneself. If the child is constantly criticized and if mistakes
are never tolerated, then the child learns to be self-critical
and hateful toward oneself. Many children are raised with
a "Be perfect" message. Since they cannot always be perfect, they are failures, and as failures something is terribly
wrong with them.

All this is not to infer that one should be blind and irresponsible toward one's limitations and mistakes. The attitude of self-love is understanding that all have limitations and make mistakes. It is even possible to make deliberate mistakes or to harm someone deliberately. It is normal to have some feelings and thoughts of hatred, revenge and anger. It is normal to hurt others and be hurt by others. It is even normal to die—so limited we are. From within this attitude we can look at our shortcomings, failures, mistakes and sins. We can look at them honestly without denying any aspect of them. And in so doing we can see how to learn from them so as to act differently if the occasion occurs again.

Those who have an attitude of self-acceptance can see all this with feelings of self-understanding, forgiveness and compassion. Those who have an attitude of self-contempt will partially (if not fully) deny their failures and limitations. Associated with a lack of complete honesty will be feelings of confusion, condemnation, anger and some sort of despair or depression. People raised to be self-rejecting can be helped by family reconstruction. The following example illustrates this point in a rather dramatic way. As I tell the story notice the different ways acceptance is given to the Explorer.

Sally was a 50-year-old woman who during her family reconstruction refused to take in any information and pictures that differed from her old perceptions. After struggling through her paternal and maternal families, I stopped the family reconstruction and told her that I wanted to check with the group to see if my gyroscope was accurate. I told Sally and the group that it seemed that every time a scene or feeling was portrayed that differed from Sally's preconceived notion, she would resist that new picture. All the group members reported that they also saw Sally doing precisely that.

According to Sally's perception of herself and of her family, everyone was poverty-stricken and unhappy; she *felt* poor and deprived even though in reality she knew she wasn't. Her mother and father, people of the soil, were born in Austria. The role players demonstrated happiness in having children and in their village and church festivals. Sally refused to believe they could be happy.

As I look back I realize I should have known that this would happen; in the interview she raised the fear that the group would disapprove of her if she made no changes. We dealt with that in great detail, assuring her that if she didn't change we would accept her anyway, and that it was obviously terribly important for her to hang on to her old deprived way of seeing herself.

In spite of Sally's resistance to new pictures, we all wanted to complete the family reconstruction. I told Sally that I wanted her to sit on the sofa, to take a few breaths and relax. I asked her to give up struggling with the scenes as they unfolded. From now on she was to simply watch a movie, not taking it in any further than just behind her eyes. I drew a line with my finger down the side of her face right beside her eyes as I said this. I told her that all I would ask of her was a very brief critique of the movie after it was over.

From then on I stayed halfway across the room from her (I had been standing close to her). I wanted to withdraw my energy from her, so she could be alone in taking in the movie. I became the director of the movie, leaving Sally to withdraw from an active role in the family reconstruction.

I then continued. We were at the point when Sally's mother and father first met each other. The role players had their "romantic" exchanges in the Austrian forests, eventually married and came to America. As each of the children of this new marriage were born, I told the family to sculpt themselves into scenes that seemed appropriate. The third child born was Sally.

The child after Sally came two years later. This birth resulted in the death of both the mother and the baby. The three remaining children were placed in an orphanage. The person role playing Sally reported continuously that she felt abandoned, deprived and full of fear. The other two children reported different reactions.

Then the father went to Austria to marry a stepmother for the three children; he brought his new wife back and reunited the family. Within a year Sally's father and step-mother had a child of their own—a boy (the first three were girls). Again, at each new stage of development in the family, I asked each role player for his or her reactions. Sally's reaction continued to be one of feeling deprived and scared, while the other two girls had different reactions.

At the birth of the baby boy I asked the family to sculpt themselves again. I asked the person playing Sally to think of what she must do to lessen her fright. I invited her to move. She left her position (clinging to her two sisters) and slowly moved over to where her father, stepmother and the new baby were. She put one of her father's hands on her. I asked her how she felt; she reported she felt less scared.

Then I asked Sally what kept her from moving over to her father. She said that if she did approach him, it would give him pleasure and she didn't want to do that! This revealed a repressed anger toward him and a spirit of revenge not to give him any pleasure.

I then asked Sally to move again to lessen the fright in her. She moved over and snuggled next to her father and touched the new half-brother. She reported her fear was lessened but again she felt resistance to do this as it would give even more pleasure to her father.

I asked Sally if she had any fear left; she said yes. So I asked her to do what she could to get rid of all the fear. She then put herself between her father and stepmother, embracing both and letting them embrace her. She reported all her fear gone. I pointed out that in being affectionate with her father she had given up her anger and revenge; indeed she had given him pleasure. I asked Sally what she wanted to do—keep her fear and revenge and deny pleasure to her father or give him pleasure and lose her fear and revenge? She left her father's side, returned to her sisters, and said she again felt afraid. I said, ''So this is your choice, not to give your father any pleasure even though you will be scared for your entire life.''

I then announced that the movie was over. During all of this I noticed the real Sally absorbed in the movie, nodding her head frequently throughout the scenes. I invited the role players to share their feelings, then deroled group members and asked if anyone wanted to share briefly what they gained for themselves from the day as we didn't have much time. Few did as it was getting late. Sally gave her brief critique of the movie.

As the group was breaking up to depart, Sally came up to me and while intently staring into my eyes said, ''What shall I do? Shall I take all that in or not?'' I said that was up to her—whatever she did would be okay, she knew best. I told her I certainly understood how she came to feel so deprived because in many ways she in fact was deprived— losing her mother, then losing her father when put into an orphanage, then losing the new relationships in the orphanage upon his return, then having to share him with a new wife, then losing her baby position in the family with the birth of her half-brother. I told her how frightening all this is to a little girl and how easy it is for a little girl to blame Daddy. Little girls just don't have the mature mind to see the full reality. I told her that if she wanted to hold onto the old pictures, it was okay by me—and I meant it: Better perhaps for Sally to give up the struggle to change and relax with the old way of seeing herself.

When the group reconvened the following month for another member's family reconstruction, Sally asked me if I had told her it was okay not to change as a trick. (Having been in therapy for nine years with one therapist after another, she was very sophisticated in all forms of therapy, including the use of paradox.) I said no.

Then Sally asked, ''Did you think that by telling me not

to change I would change?'' I said that I was aware of two things. First, I was sincere in telling her it was okay with me if she did not change because I felt that perhaps on some deep level it might not be good for her to change. Perhaps she needed to keep her old pictures and self-identity; perhaps it was too scary, too threatening, to change now. In some way her old pictures served her. I needed to respect her as she was, with whatever might be going on deep inside that I couldn't see.

Second, I told her, I also knew that often when a person is told not to change or that it is okay not to, she in fact does change. I knew that as a fact of experience. Whether it would happen to her I didn't know, but I didn't tell her this just to manipulate or trick her into change.

Then I said to Sally, ''I sincerely am trusting of you, Sally, and I sincerely do want you to know that it is okay if you don't change.'' I told her, ''Not changing may be far better for you than changing. I'm trusting that on some level you know yourself far better than I. If you don't change, your old way is serving you and is okay for you.''

A great sense of relief emanated from Sally. I was authentically validating her as she was. This was contrary to the way she had been treating herself for all these years. She had been condemning herself. She had been demanding of herself to change. Paradoxically she had not changed. If Sally decides to accept herself as is, drop the demand to change, *she will be changing in that very direction.* This will lead to further changes.

I want to close by adding a note about straight communication. Simply being straight and fully open in my communication with Sally, without shading any of my feelings or thoughts for whatever reason (such as to protect her or to protect myself) was my own way of being self-accepting. If I hide some feeling or thought of mine then the embedded message is that something is wrong with that feeling or thought and *therefore something is wrong with me.*

As I ask Sally to be fully honest with me, I am validating

all that is in her. As I let her know that I can handle and accept any feelings of anger or dislike, I am saying I accept her as she is with all of her parts. To the degree I don't want to know all of her feelings and thoughts, and subtly encourage her to tell me only the "good" things, then I am saying I don't accept her negative thoughts and feelings.

This is a crucial point. Any communication that is not fully open carries the hidden meaning that something is not acceptable to others and to myself. This is why in a family reconstruction one of the operating principles is to encourage congruent communication. It is critical that the Guide be honest. All this does not imply that there is no place for privacy. There is no rule that we must always express ourselves. But even here we can be honest, with phrases such as "It is my private business," "I don't want to tell you," "I don't have the energy or time now."

So any communication that is open and honest is a statement of self-acceptance, while any that is partially hidden can be a statement of self-rejection. Since a family reconstruction encourages congruent communication both within the family scenes and within the group, it is a marvelous process to help the Explorer face the paradox, "He who accepts himself as he is will change and he who must change will stay as he is."

Family reconstruction then takes the Explorer through two basic paradoxes of life: "He who seeks his life will lose it and he who loses his life will find it" and "He who is driven to change (due to self-rejection) will not change, and he who accepts self as is will change" or "Love your enemy (within and without)."

12

GOALS OF A FAMILY RECONSTRUCTION AND QUALITIES OF A COMPETENT GUIDE

At this point it may be helpful to summarize the goals to be achieved from a family reconstruction. Some of these are final goals (for example, raising self-esteem), and others are instrumental goals or means to the final goals. Some may seem similar to others and indeed they are, but they are different enough and important enough to be delineated as separate goals. This listing is not necessarily in the order of importance.

GOALS

1) To achieve higher self-esteem. Perhaps the loftiest goal is to help the Explorer achieve higher self-esteem. As we have seen in Chapters 2 and 9, many factors in a family reconstruction contribute to the raising of the Explorer's self-esteem.

2) To empower the Explorer. While empowering the Explorer is closely aligned to self-worth, it is only one of many factors contributing to high self-esteem. Empowerment means that, at the end of the day and as the results of the family reconstruction continue to percolate throughout the following months, the Explorer becomes less dependent on others for his or her self-esteem and more dependent on self. The Explorer actually feels more power and control operating within, as well as more confidence and courage in daily life.

True empowerment leads the Explorer to get more of his or her wants and needs met. The sense of being weak and buffeted by outside forces diminishes.

3) To have a new experience of the maternal and paternal families and of the family of origin. The emphasis of this goal is on having a *new* experience. If the Explorer simply reexperiences these families in the old familiar way, then little is accomplished. New experiences will inevitably emerge unless the Explorer resists new pictures and information. For example, most Explorers know more about one family than another (the maternal family may be more familiar than the paternal). The family reconstruction brings to light much about the least known family, so empty gaps are filled in. Also, so many of our family experiences occurred during childhood—when we were incapable of understanding what was really happening. Being mature, the Explorer can see more of the nuances and subtleties of the family transactions and of the family members themselves.

4) To immerse the Explorer in the action so that he or she relives certain critical scenes in a new way. This is similar to goal 3 but emphasizes a different objective. By watching the scenes unfold, like watching a play, the Explorer can have a new experience of the family. This fourth goal emphasizes thrusting the Explorer into the action of the play from time to time, coming up onto the stage as it were, to get into the action. This should be done at those points where the Explorer needs to redo a scene to get a *different learning* from it. The original action produced a dysfunctional rule, meaning, or way of coping with threat. The reconstructed action allows the Explorer to learn a new way or meaning.

5) To enable the Explorer to see mother and father as persons rather than roles. As long as one's parents are seen and related to as parents rather than as humans, the power of the original learnings is maintained. When an Explorer see his or her parents as human as he, then the Explorer feels an equality and similarity with mother and father. Thus, the original power held by parents over children is dispelled. This also helps the Explorer break hardened, one-sided, unreal perceptions (such as a parent being all perfect, all bad, totally irresponsible, all good, etc.). Thus, the parents are moved from being gods or devils to the status of being human with strengths and weaknesses just like the Explorer.

6) To bring about reconciliation with self-protection where estrangement exists. This goal, very closely associated with goal 5, goes one step farther. Often this cannot be accomplished within the time frame of one day's journey, but enough change may occur to allow this to happen later.

7) To zero in on unfinished business. This goal gives direction to the family reconstruction. The scenes reenacted may be determined by the unfinished business of the Explorer (for example, the Explorer may have some deep suppressed anger toward a parent, or may be terrified by the sexuality of the opposite sex). This will influence the Guide to look for opportunities during the family reconstruction to deal with these issues.

8) To substitute congruence for incongruence. One of the major dysfunctional dynamics in any family system is communication that is concealed or contradictory in its message. Whenever this appears in the family reconstruction, one of the goals is to redo the scene using congruent communication so the Explorer can experience how different that would have been. Getting the alter ego and the Explorer to substitute leveling communication for dysfunctional communication is an important goal of a family reconstruction.

9) *To help the Explorer see that changing parents and other family members is not essential, but changing self is.* During most family reconstructions, the Guide will see that the Explorer unconsciously slips into putting more energy in getting the parents to change than in changing self. Thus the goal is to let the Explorer see that this is not where the essential action needs to be. To invest more energy in getting parents to change carries the hidden message, "If only you will change I'll be happy" or "It's your fault I am what I am," which blames and thereby avoids personal responsibility.

10) *To move the Explorer from needing acceptance from others to achieving self-acceptance.* This is one aspect of goal nine but so essential that I state it as a goal in itself for clarity's sake. This is achieved often in a family reconstruction when the Explorer accepts his or her parents as they are. To be able to accept oneself is at the heart of self-esteem.

11) *To fill in missing parts.* If an Explorer sees his or her family as humorless, then somehow humor needs to be added during the family reconstruction; if anger is missing, then somehow anger needs to be added; if sexuality is missing, then somehow that needs to be added. Whenever an Explorer is adopted the biological parents must be given heavy emphasis, even though the Explorer may want to spend all the time with the adopted parents. Reenacting the presence and actions of the biological parents always has a powerful effect on an adopted Explorer; this adds his real roots!

QUALITIES

Now I would like to summarize what I think is required to be a competent Guide for a family reconstruction. This is pertinent to those aspiring to be guides and to those desiring to choose a Guide to lead them through a family reconstruction. Some of these qualities should be found in any therapist or in anyone involved in helping others to grow as humans. I will briefly list what I think those general qualities are since this is covered in much of the literature in the field. Then I will spend more time on those qualities I deem unique to the family reconstruction process.

General Qualities

1) To have true love and respect toward the Explorer, honoring his or her personhood and being truly solicitous for the Explorer's well-being.

2) To be skilled in the faculty of being observant—a veritable Sherlock Holmes.

3) To be experienced in life and in the arena of helping people grow.

4) To be in touch with self, which enables the Guide to be honest with his or her own feelings and thoughts, to be empathetic, and to be able to apply oneself appropriately.

5) To trust one's intuition and hunches, especially when the Guide is feeling good about him or herself.

6) To be able to stay objective rather than getting subjectively triggered into one's own personal material or hangups by what takes place in the family reconstruction.

7) To be able to express oneself clearly and honestly.

8) To realize that in guiding a family reconstruction mistakes can happen and failure is possible; to have the capacity to own up to those mistakes and to be accepting of oneself in the process.

9) To have the following set of beliefs:

- that 95 to 98 percent of the time people are trying to do the best they can;
- that any acting-out is merely an attempt to protect oneself from a perceived threat;
- that what a person does serves some purpose and can be the basis of transformation;

- that every human trait bears the seed of the opposite, which is a basis for transformation (for example, blaming has the seed of protecting one's interest, being sensitive bears the seed of being overly hurt);
- that within each person is the basic design and dynamic to grow humanly, that somewhere within each person is the need to be loved, respected, understood, held, reconciled, etc., even when all the data suggest the opposite;
- that basically a person heals him or herself; others do not heal the person—they only facilitate self-growth and healing;
- that change and growth are a process, that not everything has to be done in one day or with this Guide.

All these beliefs help the Guide to be trusting and accepting of the Explorer.

Qualities Related to Being a Guide in a Family Reconstruction

10) To know the process of a family reconstruction. This includes the various steps, dynamics, goals and operational principles that are set forth in this book.

11) To be continually decontaminating oneself from one's own family of origin so that in leading a family reconstruction the Guide will not be thrown off by or triggered into one's personal family. Having done one's own family reconstruction helps a Guide stay clear of his or her own family issues. The family as such offers its own set of problems differing from what may be considered individual problems.

This is an important difference and illustrated by a person who came to me hoping to do his family reconstruction. He had been in individual therapy for several years, and he himself counseled others. When it came his turn to do his family reconstruction, he refused. A year later he joined another of my groups and again refused when his turn came. His family experience was so painful that he did not want to see it as one might in a family reconstruction. In his own therapy he was dealing with *individual* issues even though many were related to the family. But dealing with the family as a *system* was another thing for this man.

12) To be able to think in terms of systems. There is a great difference between those who see, think and feel systematically and those who operate individually or psychoanalytically. The first sees that systems need to be dealt with, the second sees that only the individual needs to be dealt with. A systems person will see the entire family, the other will see only individual persons. A systems therapist takes into account how the system is always affecting the person in the here and now as well as how the person is affecting the system. The systems person looks to the social dynamics as well as internal psychological dynamics. It is interesting to see how these two types deal differently with the family. Once at a family therapy conference I witnessed a psychoanalytically oriented person work with a family. The interventions were with each person sequentially and the therapist did not check how the other family members were reacting to the individual pieces of therapy. On other occasions, I witnessed a therapist with a social worker orientation who would always check the reactions occurring in the system to any piece of work being done with a family member and deal with that. A systems therapist has no problems in seeing a client's family members even though the therapist may have spent several months alone with the client. Many individually oriented therapists have problems doing that.

13) To have the qualities of a dramatist. Since a family reconstruction is a series of psychodramatic scenes acted out (verbally, or in the silhouette of sculpting, or in pantomime) by a cast of characters, the Guide needs to have a flair for the dramatic, including an active, wide-ranging imagination, a sense of humor, a quickness of spontaneous creativity, a respect for the flow of action as well as for the rhythms of crescendo and diminuendo, a sense of timing, a capacity to see things on several different levels, the ability to take in the entire scene and then to seize the emotional moment.

14) To know the difference between directing the process and directing the person. The task of the Guide is to be in control of the process in such a way as to allow those in the scenes to be free to be themselves. The Guide does not direct the actors; the characters contribute their own material. In other words, the Guide doesn't know the plot, the actors' lines, whether the outcome will be a comedy or a tragedy. The Guide is not a theatrical director. In fact, as the family reconstruction develops, even the original goals of the Explorer may shift, as the drama reveals deeper issues unknown to the consciousness of the Explorer. The goals of a family reconstruction are general in nature, some being final and others being instrumental. Within those generalized goals the unique dynamics and context of each family can be expressed. So while the generalized goals stated above are the same for every family reconstruction, the particular goals of an Explorer, the expressions of family members, and the dynamics of each family reveal the uniqueness of each family and each Explorer. Each family reconstruction from this viewpoint is different.

In this way guiding a family reconstruction is easy. The Guide does not have to be an expert in all the ramifications of family dynamics, nor have years of experience to be able to spot common trends fitting certain types of families. The Guide does not need to analyze all the essential issues of a family beforehand and then direct all the work around that issue. If the process is guided appropriately, the cast of role players will bring out the essential elements and dynamics of the unique family system.

13 THE SPLENDOR OF BEING IN A FAMILY RECONSTRUCTION GROUP

In Chapter 4 I mention various ways to form a group in which a family reconstruction is done. One of these ways is to get some 12 to 15 people to meet on a regular basis, usually once a month. The group lasts as long as it takes to do each member's family reconstruction. This experience is very special for the Guide and for all the members of the group. The following is a description written by a person who was a member of such a group that I co-led with Anne, my wife, several years ago:

"In belonging to a family reconstruction group you take a monthly journey deep into the life of one person and that person's family. Each month you live in a family that is unique and you wonder at the mystery of how different, and yet how similar, every family is. By letting yourself go—being free with your feelings and fantasies, intuitions and insights—you have an experience of *actually living* through the uniquely fascinating blend of love and hatred, fear and courage, life and death, joy and sorrow, doubt and clarity, hope and disappointment, ying and yang, light and shadow, good and evil, rejection and forgiveness that makes up all of life itself.

"By doing this, you take a day out of your busy life to concentrate your energies into experiencing and reflecting on the major themes of your life and the lives of each person in the group. In this way you enter into the sacred in an experiential and contemplative way. Your heart is sensitized and your soul is deepened. Entering into the deepest levels of your spirit there is the

161

chance of touching the mysterious and responding with a sigh of gratefulness and a "yes" to life itself. You feel empowered and fragile at the same time, aware of your connection to all around you, of your need for others and what you give to them.

"You begin to grow more and more into knowing what trust can be like as each month person after person opens his or her life to the rest. The specialness and sacredness of that person are given to your care and safe-keeping, as indeed you come to offer yourself in the same way.

"Softness, tenderness, strength and sensitivity grow in each person and in the group. You return home knowing that life does conquer death, love overcomes resentment and even hatred, mercy is on the other side of hardness, and that each person in the world regardless of endowments is precious as a flower and to be held in deepest, religious respect. The marvel of this human person is monthly unfolded before your very eyes, ears, breath and body in a way that makes you feel larger than life itself.

"All this growth comes to the degree you can let yourself go and enter into the experience with all your energy and courage and love. It is a transcending of your accustomed boundaries of existence."

Members derive great benefit from a family reconstruction group even when they are not doing their own family reconstruction. Usually being in a role is the best way for a member to benefit. The mere fact that he or she is chosen for a role indicates that some characteristics in that person are similar to the family member being portrayed. Thus, the stirrings that occur in one's thoughts and feelings while in that role may have a direct bearing on one's own life.

Benefits can and often do occur even to those who are not chosen to play a role, who simply sit there watching the action unfold. The following is a description written by a group member who was on the sidelines during a family reconstruction and what happened to him:

"Well!

"Yesterday afternoon the dam broke. Like the bluebird, in the twinkling of an eye. And the flood continues, letting out 40 years of bottled-up feelings.

"At the end of Betty's family reconstruction, Anne, co-guiding with Bill, asked us to conjure up an image of our fathers. I got into perfect touch with my father, and discussed with him many of the learnings from the reconstruction. I was suffused with happiness, as if back at age 12 and traveling with him in the car, all over the Midwest.

"Then I had to say goodbye to my father, and Anne said to do the same thing with my mother. My body stiffened and refused. I opened my eyes and stared at the floor while others spoke with their mothers. (It was like Betty unable to talk to her mother during the family reconstruction.) I held myself tight and rigid, the words in my mind were 'You can/must endure it one more time.'

"Then Anne said to end the visit and conjure up a good friend. I released my body and closed my eyes, but instead of a friend, a vivid image intruded itself into my visual field—a dark, round hole surrounded by a ring of dim light. Part of my mind instructed me—in a loving, reassuring way—to stay with it and refine the image. Step by step, the image refined itself until I suddenly saw that it was a vagina. At the same instant, I got the clear sentence (not from A, but from another voice, B): *'You may be your sister's father.'*

"Along with this message came an envelope (from A) saying: *'You can handle this now.'*

"Miscellaneous facts came flooding in, but the strongest feeling was *'Oooooh, that's* what I was hiding.' I had never even suspected it, because it was hidden behind the vagina image (hidden by me, of course, when I was 12 years old). Some background on this. About three years ago, I had learned under hypnosis that I had been abused by my mother. I had always known to some extent about verbal abuse, which continued into adulthood, but I had suppressed the physical abuse. Under the same hypnosis, I had learned that there was some sort of sexual abuse as well, but he could not get me past a very strong wall that I had built to hide the nature of that abuse from me. I've been trying to get behind it ever since, with only partial success. Now I see why, and could reconstruct so many loose pieces from my life. As a young boy, I knew that my mother was doing something sexual with me, and somehow I got the idea that when she got pregnant, I could have been the father. (And perhaps I could—I was a precocious 12-year-old, but those details don't matter now, 40 years later.) In any case, I somehow got the message that this was something I could *never tell anyone*—which is probably a pretty sensible rule, when you consider what would have happened to me and our family if it came out that I was my sister's father, or even might be. Now it doesn't seem to matter much.

"The most interesting phenomenon connected with this revelation is my feeling of *amusement*. How silly to carry a misimpression from a 12-year-old's understanding of sex for 40 years, or a correct impression that can't have any useful survival value for a 50-year-old. There are so many distortions in areas of my life that had to be made to fit that 12-year-old's decision. Some ideas and pieces that show how the family reconstruction brought it out in me:

"1) When we were preparing for the reconstruction, I completely resisted the idea of filling in the unknown areas of my family data, even when we were encouraged to do so. A dominant theme in my family was lying to cover up dark secrets. Then the secrets theme came up in Betty's reconstruction, which I recognized because she had picked me out several months earlier after the group had begun as someone she could tell a dark secret to. I learned it well, and it showed. However, I didn't want to contribute to that tradition anymore.

"2) All my life I had studied *everything* I could find about sex and sexual abuse, as if trying to discover a dark secret, but nothing ever helped until this final moment, when all this cognitive information was available to correct all the accumulated junk in the twinkling of an eye. In Betty's reconstruction, I identified with her 91-year-old grandfather role player, and I had developed the feeling of a person able to look over an entire family history and recall it from my mind. This helped the process of recovering all my own blanked-out information.

"3) All this reconstructed information ties in with my attitudes and feelings about being 'forced' to do anything, especially by a woman. This happened in the group when it seemed to me Anne was taking the lead in deciding who was to do family reconstructions in the months to come. I very much resented her process. It was strange how I did this as obviously Bill was part of the process, but I singled out Anne to resent.

"4) After the reconstruction, I was opened up to dozens of things, mostly through things that just keep popping into my head. It's now a week later and it's still going on. It's as if I've opened up sealed pages of the family book. And my feelings toward my mother are simply sadness for her that she couldn't do any better, and probably never understood what she was doing, any more than I knew what I was covering up.

"That's it, sparing you some of the details. I wonder what would have turned up if I'd actually been the Explorer in the reconstruction! It seems to me I *was* the Explorer."

Another example of how group members benefit is described in the following account by a lady of some 70 years of age:

"In the past, I have given lip service to the value for persons role-playing members of another's family in family restructuring, but it was not until Bill Nerin's workshop in March that I experienced first-hand that value.

"Cynthia asked me to role-play her grandmother in her sculpted family. I accepted unhesitatingly, but when she described the grandmother as a paranoid schizophrenic I realized with a shock that she was describing my own mother. I knew it was going to be difficult to play a paranoid schizophrenic, violent, rejecting, and physically and emotionally abusive grandmother.

"As I got into the role, however, I began to understand as never before my own mother's desperate need to hold on to her husband, and her viewing of her two daughters as rivals for his affection and, therefore, a threat to her. I felt some of my mother's desperation, when in the psychodrama the grandfather role player distanced himself from my jealous possessiveness. I felt some of my mother's fear that her outrageous behavior was driving away the one person she most needed: her husband. I felt some of her rage and fear provoked by the husband's giving of affection and love to the girls.

"After this 'sculpt' ended, Bill mentioned the word 'fear,' and

I thought: Yes, that was what I was feeling, as I got into the role of the 'grandmother' so much like my own mother. Had that been the main emotion felt by my mother, all those years while I was growing up, terrified of her?

"Driving home after the workshop's first day, I thought more about this, and, for the first time ever, I began to feel pity for my mother; I even said aloud the words, 'Poor little thing!' (She was a tiny woman.) I had a feeling of release, of freedom from something. But freedom from what? Then I realized I was free, after seventy years of anger toward my mother, to give up that anger, and to reclaim the energy it had taken to keep it alive. I could feel compassion, and deep sadness for the way her terrors affected the lives of my father, my sister, and myself. Then, because the anger didn't dominate everything, I could look at what she had given me that I could value. This was difficult, but it came to me that she had taught me to love beautiful music, fine art; and she had taught me good manners. Not in a structured way, but simply by continually exposing me to them. I actually said aloud, 'Thank you for these, Mother.'

"Many times I have prayed that God would help me stop hating my mother; I didn't want to waste energy hating anyone! Finally God did, through Bill Nerin."

These are sterling examples of how a person, being open and motivated, can identify with the characters in a family reconstruction and get drawn into the drama so as to achieve enormous personal breakthroughs.

The value of a family reconstruction group grows as the months unfold. Great trust and caring develop among the group members. The members share what has been happening in their lives. Victories are celebrated and misfortunes are felt with sadness. In some ways it is like an Alcoholics Anonymous group, but the subject is family and personal life rather than the disease of alcoholism. The group is a support for members, enabling them to unlock the families within and to free the self to go on to higher self-worth.

14 FAMILY RECONSTRUCTION IN OTHER THERAPEUTIC SETTINGS

The principles underlying family reconstruction and the techniques used in a family reconstruction can be used in settings other than a therapeutic group of 10 or more. One such setting is in the area of education. A mini reconstruction can be enacted with a great deal of humor to teach a class or audience of people how the five basic learnings described in Chapter 2 are learned from one's family.

My wife Anne uses this effectively in teaching. She will get people from the audience to play the roles of a mother, a father and a two-year-old child. The scene is Thanksgiving dinner. The parents' families are invited. Anne then gets role players for each of these families. She tells the family of the young mother that they are very straight-laced and rigid. The family of the young father is instructed to be loose and not into being "proper." Anne also adds that the young father has a brother who loves to drink and the mother has a sister who is hard of hearing.

The role players enact the scene with much fun and gusto; you can imagine what takes place. The mother's family usually arrives on time and through the front door, and the father's family usually arrives late and through the kitchen door. The drama goes on from there—it becomes a mini Archie Bunker scenario. After 30 minutes Anne solicits from the two-year-old all of her reactions. As she reports her experience, it is easy to see how the rigid and loose learnings of her mother and father are assimilated. The patterns of communication and coping, the rules and sets of meanings are seen developing in the child.

Anne has developed another way to use the principles of family reconstruction in an educational setting. At PTA-type meetings she divides those attending into four groups: those who are first-born, those who are middle-born, those who are the youngest, and those who are only children. Then she asks one person in each group to be the recording secretary and write down what is said while the others discuss growing up in their families. When the reports are made to the entire group, it is striking how the experience was different for each group and within each group the experience was so similar: The first-born felt more responsibility and had to set an example for the others; the youngest felt younger than their actual age and found the process of growing up was slow; the middle children felt more relaxed; and only children felt adult early on.

What is even more astonishing is that, as the subgroups report back to the entire group, an interaction occurs among the groups illustrating the sibling rivalry that occurs between children of different birth order! Every family reconstruction reveals this phenomenon and can help a person understand what may be going on between that person and one's siblings in adult life, even though they may be in their seventies.

Within the therapeutic setting the elements of family reconstruction can be used in countless ways. The mere recording of a client's three family trees, as illustrated in Chapter 3, carries the message to the client that no matter what the issue, it is connected in some way to family roots. This unconsciously gives a larger explanation for the client's dilemma, removing the stinging notion that it is totally the result of the self. The family trees will also give the therapist hunches that may be important to follow. If the client is the only girl in the midst of four brothers, if a female client carries the name of her father, if a sibling died prior to the client's birth, if divorce occurred early in the child's life, if the parents quickly remarried after divorcing—all these greatly influence the development of personality.

The basic principle here is that the acting-out of the client is most likely connected with his or her coping with being threatened, with the stress of surviving. This threat to survival and the way to deal with it originates in the family of origin. The family trees directly address this issue.

This principle of coping with survival is obviously dealt with in a family reconstruction. In dealing with a client on a one-to-one basis in my office, I'll often ask the client to sculpt me as the father and herself as the mother to illustrate how the parents were when she (or he) was growing up. Then I'll have the client sculpt me in the child's position. Often this leads to the heart of the threat and what is still going on in adult life. Then I ask the client to take the child's position, imagine the sculpt of the mother and father (I remain in the father's sculpt), and then deal with the threat in a new way, getting what she needs for herself as that child. Finally, I recreate her present dilemma through a sculpt and have her deal with that in a new way (usually the way reenacted as the child).

In this example, a principle of family systems is revealed through family reconstruction and a technique from family reconstruction is used—in an office setting. This is even easier if I am treating a client with a woman co-therapist, or if the client is there with her spouse, her loved one, or members of her family. The client then has the opportunity to use the other people in the sculpt.

When Anne or I deal with a couple or a family, we strongly encourage them to see both of us. We have found that the therapy is quicker, more incisive and richer in opportunities. We are able to ask each partner to sculpt us as he, then she, sees the relationship. We do this in the first session. They are surprised as they hear us report what we are feeling and thinking! They have given us little or no history,

little or no description of their problem, yet here we are
understanding the basic dynamics of the issue. You can imagine the trust this builds in them toward us some 30 minutes into the first session.

If time permits in the first session, and certainly in the
second session, we ask clients we are treating to sculpt us
as each would like the relationship to be. Then we ask them
to assume each one's original sculpt of the way the relationship currently is and move very slowly, without talking, to
a sculpt of the way they want the relationship to be. We ask
each of them to track what goes on inside as they slowly
move from the present to the future, what fears they encounter, what obstacles they overcome, what it takes for
them to get to their ideal relationship.

After both spouses do their two sculptures, moving slowly from the first to the second, we ask them to report what
their journey was like, what it took for them to get where
they wanted to be. Often this provides the essential material
for the therapeutic process. If the issue is deeply buried, we
ask them to sculpt their mothers, fathers and themselves as
they grew up. Within these scenes of origin we can often
unlock the stuck position in which the clients find themselves.

Again, the use of sculpting, of going to the family of
origin, of using the internal journey of pantomime movement are techniques used in family reconstruction. The technique of going back to the families of origin, where the learnings originated, in this psychodramatic way is an effective
method of using family reconstruction with two or four people in an office setting. Even simply having a client do the
family reconstruction homework—the family trees, the chronology, the circle of influence and the birth fantasies—will
prove to be very rewarding to the client and the therapeutic
process.

Often I have a client use fantasy to reconstruct scenes that
we would have done live in a family reconstruction. In other
words, instead of using sculpting as the vehicle to create

scenes, I use fantasy. The following example is interesting because it is directly tied to a family reconstruction that had been done a year before. Chris, whose report is found in Chapter 1, came to see me about a year after his family reconstruction. He said he wanted to talk about dating. He was beginning to worry that he would never get close to women. After talking briefly about his dating pattern, I told him I wanted to guide him through some fantasies. I induced a deep hypnotic state and had him be a small boy in a concrete scene in which he had to tell his mother that he didn't want to do something she wanted of him. I told him to do the same in a scene with his beloved grandmother (his mother's mother) and then in a scene with a date.

I felt it was important to have Chris relate to all three types of women; the date represented the present, the mother was very likely the one from whom Chris learned his rule of survival, and the grandmother was the one with whom he lived out this rule. Even if I had not suspected this, I would have included the three women, as they were all three significantly involved in his life. After he conjured up his three fantasies, he reported that saying no to his mother and to his date was easy, but it was very difficult to say no to his grandmother. With her he felt enormously guilty and selfish, as she began to feel hurt by his refusal to go along with what she wanted.

I told Chris to go back into his fantasy and tell his mother about this problem he was having with his grandmother, to see what his mother's reaction would be. He felt better when he imagined hearing his mother say, "Don't worry," but yet he still felt obligated to do the bidding of his grandmother. Then I had him go back into the fantasy and tell his mother what he had just told me about still feeling obligated, and to pay close attention to each transaction in the scene. "Be honest with your mother," I advised, "and express every feeling and reaction you are having in the conversation with her and see where it goes."

After a very long time, Chris opened his eyes and told

me his mother got very defensive with him. "She doesn't understand why I can't accommodate my grandmother," he said, "and why I feel guilty. I got mad at her and the whole situation, yelled at her and walked out." In this scene Chris broke the rule of survival by confronting the powerful parent. He was not able to do this during his family reconstruction.

I then had Chris fantasize going to his father the next day to tell him of his problem with his grandmother as well as what happened the day before while talking to his mother. "Get your father's reaction," I told him, "and again stay in touch with your reactions and express them openly."

After a while Chris opened his eyes and described his fantasy: "Dad said, 'Why don't you go to your grandmother's for dinner every Tuesday? That's no big deal.' I told him it was a big deal for me. I then told Dad that I'd prefer to call her and tell her when I'm coming over rather than feel obligated every Tuesday. Dad felt okay about that solution yet felt some disappointment with me. I told him I'd probably end up seeing Grandmother more often as long as I was in control of figuring out what fit for me as well as what fit for Grandmother." Chris reported feeling good about this fantasy.

I brought in the father to complete the gestalt. In every family each person plays a role in whatever is happening, and I knew it would be valuable to bring in the father even though it appeared that the dysfunctional dynamics were only among Chris and his mother and grandmother. Chris's report revealed the role of his father, which was to reinforce the rule to always make the woman happy to the point of ignoring one's own needs. In the fantasy Chris contended with his mother and father over this rule and decided for himself what action he would take! Thus Chris was able to deal with both powers setting the unreasonable rule, and so with all the factors in the system. This final resolution lead to a good feeling.

Finally, I suggested that Chris recall this fantasy in the months ahead. Some refer to this as a future pace. We then ended the session.

Here is Chris's own account of what happened to him afterwards. The particular dynamics of family reconstruction are explained in italics:

"I met with Bill a couple months ago. I don't remember exactly what the discussion was, but I imagine it had to do with my dating, my feelings of responsibility for my date, my insecurities, etc. Anyway, near the end of the session, Bill had me close my eyes and imagine a situation in which my mother and grandmother were wanting me to do something I didn't want to do. I then imagined myself telling them of my desires and wishes— and that I did not want to complete their deed."

Being in an altered state, he forgets much of what actually occurred.

"After leaving the session I remember thinking it was a useless exercise. I didn't see the point of it, nor did it seem to accomplish anything. I noticed later that day I was very tense, my face tense, and I did not feel good physically. The next few days I was depressed, felt very lonely. My stomach hurt some. I was kind of scared. I was mad and disappointed in myelf. This lasted about 10 days, slowly getting better and better. I did not know what to attribute all this to; I certainly did not connect it to the session, unless seeing Bill recreated or brought back memories of old, bad times."

By asserting himself, Chris ran the risk of not having mother's, father's and grandmother's approval. He feels lonely as he severed the way he was relating to his grandmother and entered into a new kind of relationship. As the new way of relating takes hold, Chris begins to feel better.

"Two months later I met with Bill. He asked me if anything had happened after our session. I said no. About 30 minutes later it dawned on me that I began feeling bad right after the session and that at this point I felt better than I had in years. I relayed this to him. It all began to make sense. That session had apparently done a lot more than I had ever imagined.

"Family reconstruction has always puzzled me. What is the mechanism by which it works? Psychologically, how?

"Well, that session revealed a lot of the power of the unconscious. How it works I don't know, but very obviously something during that fantasy released something that actually affected my physical and psychological being. I felt both mentally and physically terrible for about two weeks following that session and at the time had no idea why. I was disappointed in myself. Then slowly I got stronger and better; since that time I've felt physically and mentally very, very good, very strong."

This case illustrates many points. First, it is an example of using material from a client's original family reconstruction. I knew from his reconstruction that Chris had this central issue of making his grandmother happy. To please others, especially women, seemed to be Chris's basic rule of survival. So in my later session with Chris concerning his inability to be close with women, I could go immediately back to the scenes in Chris's family reconstruction. This illustrates how the family reconstruction itself only began a process. The fantasy work carried Chris's progress a significant step further.

This case is also a particularly powerful example of the value of fantasy. The two weeks of feeling low and lonely followed by a growing sense of strength to a point where Chris claimed he had never before felt so strong reveal how the fantasy work so deeply stirred his insides.

Another use of family reconstruction is in staff consultation. Once a staff of mental health professionals invited my wife Anne to consult with them over some problems they were having among themselves. Instead of dealing with those problems head on, she suggested doing someone's family reconstruction. This seemed like a strange way to proceed. How would one person's family reconstruction solve the problems among the staff members? Trusting Anne, they agreed to spend the day doing a reconstruction rather than dealing with their immediate issues.

Several weeks later, Anne received feedback from the staff that the problems they were having somehow resolved themselves and disappeared! What could explain that? I have some possible explanations.

During the family reconstruction, the staff members—playing various roles—became very sensitive to the basic human dilemmas that all of us face at one time or another. As compassion and understanding grew for the various members of the families being portrayed, by an unconscious analogy some compassion and understanding were extended by each person to others on the staff.

Just as they could understand how various members of the three families acted in certain ways to protect themselves from threat, they could see by analogy how they as staff members acted in ways that served to protect themselves. As the family reconstruction illustrated congruent methods of relating and coping, so again the staff could see how they could be congruent among themselves.

Just as the family reconstruction enabled the Explorer to perceive her mother and father as persons rather than as roles, so the staff could begin to perceive the director, supervisor, and manager as real persons. At the end of the reconstruction each member of the staff explained how this reconstruction helped them in regard to their own families and dilemmas. A sense of community developed over the fact that each one traveled a long journey out of the womb to the present day. That sense of community was heightened during the day as the whole staff gave themselves in care and love to the Explorer doing her family reconstruction.

In summary, I think what happened that day is that each staff person experienced the dynamics of communications, rules, meanings, and coping with threats to survival within the family system. Then they could see how those dynamics were functional and dysfunctional within their own staff system. The staff in essence was involved in experiencing a day-long metaphor. It was as though the staff said to Anne, "We are having these problems," and Anne responded, "That reminds me of a story. One day . . . " And that story was the live portrayal of the Explorer's family, in which was contained all the problems and avenues of solutions of any set of humans living in a system such as the staff of the clinic.

The honest portrayal of a family system taken into several generations is such a powerful way to bond people together that I think we are not taking advantage of this reality in bringing people together. The popularity of the TV series "Roots" speaks to this truth. Family reconstruction is a psychological version of "Roots." I believe variations on the theme of family reconstruction could be imaginatively employed in all sorts of settings. Here I've given you just a few examples. The Appendix contains exercises that exemplify further uses. I hope this will stimulate your own imagination, helping you to increase your own ways of using family reconstruction.

15 ADDED POWER: MAN AND WOMAN CO-GUIDES

We are made up of many diverse psychological traits or parts. Our task is to integrate these various parts into a harmonious working order. So as we develop we need to integrate softness with toughness, intuition with logical abstraction, assertiveness with compliance, sense of self with sense of others, consistency with flexibility, sexual passion with tenderness. One of the most common problems I encounter in this area is that of integrating the female and male parts within us. It is a never-ending task.

A manifestation of this difficulty is seen in the social and psychological phenomenon of sexism, whether it is male prejudice toward women or female prejudice toward men. I contend that this age-old phenomenon is merely a reflection of the inability of a person to integrate his or her own femaleness and maleness. To the degree that a man is prejudiced toward women I suspect he is also belittling his own femaleness, and the reverse goes for women.

I further contend that this inability to integrate one's male part with the female part is due to our rearing. When a child is raised by a father and a mother who do not mutually respect each other's equality and differences, then that child is raised by a man and a woman who are not maturely together or integrated. On the other hand, when a child is reared by parents who mutually relate so as to encourage each other's personal growth, then that child is experiencing an authentic integration between the female and male.

177

Such a child has the best opportunity to achieve that interior integration of his or her male and female parts.

Since a family reconstruction is a reentry into one's childhood so as to relive it in a new and different way, it is a marvelous opportunity to be guided by a man and a woman who are themselves integrated. At this very moment of reconstructing one's family experiences, the Explorer is in the hands of two guides (symbolic parents) who exhibit a togetherness that may be a new experience for the Explorer. If so, at this very moment of intense openness, the Explorer can be reparented by a pair of co-guides who respect each other as being both equal and different. To the degree that a particular family reconstruction is a powerful experience, the unconscious is powerfully open toward integrating the Explorer's male and female parts. Thus, being co-guided is an added plus to a family reconstruction.

A good example of this occurred several years ago in the Midwest. My wife, Anne, and I were co-guiding a woman whom I shall call Jennie through her family reconstruction. Her mother had been both submissive to her father and also sexually manipulative. Both her father and mother had come from parents of the same makeup. So Jennie's mother learned to be submissive and manipulative from her mother and Jennie's father learned to be controlling from his father. Jennie was sexually abused as a child. As a result she had real problems integrating her interior male and female parts. To bring about such integration was one of her major goals in the family reconstruction.

Unwittingly she chose as her alter ego a woman who also had been sexually abused and who alternated between hating herself for being a woman and hating men. The alter ego would move toward and away from men in a steady rhythm. Jennie, not knowing this, nevertheless picked her from a group of 38 people to be her alter ego!

Later, during the family reconstruction, there was a moment when I was taking the lead in guiding with Anne nearby. Jennie's mother had seven brothers and one sister. While the group had a fair mix of men and women, Jennie nevertheless picked women to play the roles of her mother's brothers. When I lined them up in a cluster, she gasped and said, "I've picked all women to play the brothers of my mother—I'm protecting her from all those men!" Instead of suggesting that she reconsider or choose differently (and sensing a most subtle submission and hesitation toward me), I said, "Let's see what'll happen."

I asked Jennie's role-playing mother to close her eyes and be aware of what she was feeling while surrounded by her brothers (all played by women). Then with her eyes closed I quietly moved the women away and substituted all men. I asked her to open her eyes, take in her environment, close her eyes again and be aware of what she was feeling. She immediately reported that even with her eyes closed she felt overwhelmed by male energy—she knew males had been substituted even before seeing with her eyes!

I then asked Jennie what she wanted to do. She said she wanted to substitute men. After she did, I asked both Jennie and her alter ego how they felt. Jennie simply said it felt better to see her mother's brothers as men, but she was a little scared. Her alter ego said, "Bill, I really respect what you did and feel real good toward you. I was afraid you'd ask Jennie to pick men instead. I like that you simply showed what the difference was and let Jennie decide what to do." She said that in such a quiet but profoundly moving way that after the family reconstruction that one scene stuck in my mind as a very important one in helping Jennie integrate her feminine and masculine parts.

I suspect that this scene unfolded the way it did, with such an impact on Jennie, due to what was going on between Anne and me. First, Jennie had experienced our congruent give-and-take, our blending together with our individual contributions throughout the day as well as in the interview prior to the day itself. Thus she was seeing our masculine and feminine parts operate in an integrated fashion.

Secondly, I am convinced that the integrative energy that had been going on between Anne and me during the day helped sensitize me to feeling Jennie's subtle submissiveness and hesitation toward me. Sensing this I walked the path I did rather than say, "What about choosing men instead of women?" If integration had not been a large problem with Jennie, I would have sensed no fear in her and could have more directly made the suggestion to substitute men for women. Or, if I had not been integrated myself at that moment, I would have been insensitive to her needs.

Thus, I was able to respect Jennie at this critical moment when she was protecting her mother from men (protecting her interior female part from the male part). Feeling respected by me she was able to decide to unite her mother with men (uniting her feminine and masculine parts within her). I believe that my not showing any dominance—as indicated by the alter ego's statement, "Bill, I was afraid you'd ask Jennie to pick men instead"—set the atmosphere of equality between male and female. Within that atmosphere Jennie felt free to put the men with her mother. Anne's obvious acceptance and approval of all this gave additional weight to the whole experience.

Having male and female co-guides facilitates the integration of the male and female parts of the Explorer. Aside from the integrative process, there is another advantage of a family reconstruction being guided by a man and woman. In some way this joint leadership of the group process is analogous to a family system. The guides were using leadership power to nurture, protect and stimulate the process so that the people within the group can grow, just as parents do within the family.

When the female and male leaders use processes conducive to high self-worth—such as congruent communication, flexible rules, adoptable meanings, and real or leveling ways of dealing with threats and stress—then the Explorer experiences a new kind of "family" within the day's process. By introducing such open processes into the group, the Explorer has an experience that is in many ways counter to his or her original family experience. Since this experience is happening within the context of re-doing one's family, the analogue of the group is most powerful. All this goes on unconsciously. Since the guides are a female and a male, the unconscious connection to mother and father is made.

I cannot recall any Explorer or group member ever commenting on this phenomenon, but I believe it is powerfully operating. Usually members of the group will comment to Anne and me how impressed they are by how well we worked together, but never has anyone specifically made the application to the "mother-father-family" analogue.

Another advantage of a man and a woman acting as co-guides stems from the fact that none of us can completely escape the scars of being raised in a sexist society. For example, a man may have a subtle or unconscious disrespect for a woman's intellectual capacities and a woman may have an unconscious fear of being dominated by a man. Added to the scars of sexism is the biological fact that a man, not being a woman, cannot grasp certain nuances of a woman. The same goes for women with men. So when a family reconstruction is guided by both a man and a woman, they balance each other and offer to the Explorer and to the process a more complete ability to grasp all the nuances of understanding.

An extension of this advantage is the opportunity for the Explorer's own male or female bias to be addressed. For example, if a woman is biased toward men, then she can begin the family reconstruction trusting more the woman guide. If only a man guided the family reconstruction, the Explorer would have to overcome that bias to be completely open. So when Anne and I work together, we pick that up, respect that bias and know it is an issue to be dealt with on some level. As the family reconstruction develops, the biased Explorer sees the trust Anne and I have with each other, and that provides an environment for the Explorer to develop greater trust in me. When the Explorer drops her guard against me as a male and finds herself being respected by me, then she has taken one more step in dealing with that bias—and that bias may be preventing her from achieving intimacy with a man.

In co-guiding often one of the guides is in the foreground while the other is in the background. While the one in the foreground is active in the execution of the family reconstruction and is staying close to the Explorer, reading the Explorer's constant reactions, the one in the background can take in more of the total experience. The one in the background can also be feeling and thinking and intuiting on a level different from the one guiding the action of the family reconstruction, and adding these insights to the process. So often the major breakthroughs of a person's family reconstruction have come when either Anne or I, being in the background, see a deeper issue to be dealt with than what is on the surface in the action of the moment.

This does not imply that the Guide in the active leadership role cannot catch these deeper insights. Often being so close to the action, energy and feelings allows the active Guide to see something the one in the background is missing. However, having a Guide in both the foreground and background does add that special advantage to the family reconstruction.

At other times the co-guides can be equally active in leading the process. Just as two are co-guiding, so two can use themselves in creative ways other than those mentioned above. For example, one time an Explorer abruptly announced that he did not want to continue with his family reconstruction. At first we tried to get from him what was going on. It seemed as if he was so overwhelmed that he had no idea what was going on. So we asked him to sit down and take a deep breath; Anne and I sat beside him. I took the side of him that wanted to stop. I said such things as, "I can understand John. If I were him I wouldn't want to go on either. I'm feeling scared of what I might see about my father. I may have to confront him. I've never done that. He has such terrible anger, I'm so afraid his anger will erupt and *kill me*. I am ten years old here. If I tell him what's really going on he'll beat me and kill me. I know, he beat me before with his strap."

Then Anne said, "I understand how scary it is for you as a little ten-year-old boy. And I admire your sharp instinct of self-survival. Being afraid of being killed you prudently decide not to confront your dad at this moment when his rage could be ignited. Your prudence kept you from being whipped and killed. And being ten and so scared I can see how it never entered your mind to talk to your dad *at some other time* when he was in a better mood, less threatened himself. It never occurred to you to tell him how afraid you were of his anger, how that silenced you, how you wanted him not to drink so much, how it hurt you to see your mother so hurt, how threatened and guilty he must feel. Of course being ten you were not able to understand what was going on in your father under his rage, how helpless he felt."

We fell into silence. Very quietly John stood up and stated he wanted to go on. In some way we tapped into some of the feelings under his "overwhelmed" state and helped him to sort things out, appreciate himself as caring for himself at age ten, seeing that as an adult he could reconstruct the scene and go through it, sharing his honest feelings for the first time with his dad.

This dialogue between Anne and me allowed John to distance himself from his own threatened state, to see and hear it outside of himself. Then he could integrate it within. When Anne and I had earlier tried to get him to deal with the threat directly, it was too close to home, too threatening.

We gave outside expression to both sides of him, clarifying his struggle in a more removed and less threatening way. Our silence after we spoke gave him time to assimilate what we had said and to apply those aspects that fit for him. Also, we were not directly pushing him to go on.

We could have dealt with John's threat in other ways, too, like talking to the alter ego, who probably was not overwhelmed. Perhaps that alter ego could have expressed both sides of him. Or I could have stood behind John and stated his scared side and then stood behind the alter ego and stated the other side. However, I think that since John trusted Anne and me so much, the fact that the dialogue came from our lips as co-guides facilitated the change in him.

These are some of the many ways Anne and I have used ourselves creatively in therapeutic situations that would not have been ours to use had we been alone. For all these reasons, whenever an Explorer can use a woman and man as co-guides, the family reconstruction is enriched.

16 DISCOVERIES AND THEMES TO BE NOTED

As I have guided family reconstructions over the years certain themes have left a lasting impression on my mind. I have learned more about family systems by leading family reconstructions than from any other source. I would like to share these impressions with you.

A child is capable of making outlandish judgments. These judgments can persist and operate throughout one's life. An example of this is the judgment that one parent is all-good and the other all-bad. Irrational conclusions can be made over simple events—a child may conclude that she or he is not loved by a parent when the child awakens alone in the house and becomes gripped with fear. A child can conclude that mother loves brother more because she once favored brother in a fist fight. No wonder at times parents find it hard to understand their children's attitudes. "How could you have drawn that conclusion!" is an often repeated comment of parents. The immature mind can do funny things at times.

The "innocent" parent colludes in some way with the wrong-doing of the "bad" parent. For example, if one spouse is depressed, how does the other spouse participate in that? If one is a hypochondriac, what role does the other play in that? If a father is withdrawn from parenting, how does the mother participate in that? Their mutual participation is usually done through a series of happenings that eventually lead to a somewhat dysfunctional state of affairs.

For example, in the beginning a father may make some attempt to parent his infant, tentative though it may be due to his inexperience and upbringing. Then the mother sees his awkwardness, fears for the child and takes over the parenting. As this is done the father feels pushed away and even more inadequate. By the time the child is three or four years old, he notices all of the parenting is done by his mother. Father only provides the material sustenance. Then the child can hear mother complain about being fully responsible for the parenting—forgetting the rhythmic interchanges during the child's first year that resulted in the static role positions. So the child can pick up the message "Poor Mother is left to do all the work and Father is not helping as he should."

Whatever is happening within the system is brought about by everyone's participation in some way. This dynamic is similar to the one above. To return to the example of parenting, the child is also contributing to mother's parenting and father's withdrawing. A more assertive child would put greater demands on father's attention than a submissive child. You can see how the outcome is modified. So I have found it extremely important to realize that no one person is responsible for an outcome in a family. All family members in some way participate in the results produced. Therefore, no one person is to be completely blamed in a system. Each is responsible to some degree. The question is not "Who is to blame?" but rather, "How can each person assume responsibility for what is happening?"

A parent tends to get from a child what he or she is not getting from the spouse. For example, a mother may get support and "understanding" from her son or daughter if she isn't getting it from her husband. A father may get his principal satisfaction in life from his son or daughter if he is not getting it from his wife. Of course, when this happens an inappropriate and heavy burden is put on the child. Usually this goes on outside the awareness of the parent.

Everyone in a system usually and eventually profits when one person in the system goes after what he or she needs. Whenever the needs of a person within a system change and that person seeks to satisfy the emerging need, the system is disturbed. The system has learned to satisfy the old needs and gets into a habit of so behaving. So the old ways are disturbed when new needs demand new ways.

An obvious example of this is the growing child's needing greater freedom to mature. Often parents and the entire system resist this trend. As the resistance to meeting new needs hardens, often the individual (whether child or adult) gives up the struggle to get his or her needs met, but as one person's needs go unfulfilled so usually all members of the system suffer. If a child gives up and remains a "child" even though 25 years of age, the need for parents to phase through the parenting stage is never met. If the child struggles to be emancipated, the parents are forced to grow beyond parenting and to find meaning in life from other sources, which adds to their growth.

In family reconstruction I often ask the Explorer or alter ego to reach out to get his or her needs met. When this is done the Explorer sees how everyone in the family—after some struggle, disturbance and pain—eventually benefits.

Three marvelous instructions. If someone were to ask me today, "If you could teach only three lessons what would you teach?" I would answer:

1) How to go through normal emotional pain instead of distracting oneself from it, as this is an essential way to grow.

2) How to handle disagreements and threats in a constructive way.

3) That it is okay to make mistakes.

After leading person after person through family reconstructions, I see how pervasive is the tendency to avoid pain and struggle. The issue is not just that pain is painful (and, therefore, who wants it?) but that people are not taught how to deal with it in such a way as to come through it to a profitable conclusion. It is normal for parents to shield their children from pain. There are functional and dysfunctional ways to do this. A dysfunctional way is to convey the message, "Don't be in pain" (therefore pain is evil), "Don't risk to the point of pain," (take drugs or distractors not to feel it). Even therapists can get seduced into this and make therapy sessions quick fixes rather than sessions of deep healing whereby a person experiences the pain, can learn from it and know how to deal with the underlying causes.

Dealing with disagreements and threats is a special form of dealing with pain. So often people are not taught how to deal with irritations, anger and disagreements so as to arrive at solutions from which all members of the system benefit. Because so many are bereft of this teaching, blockages are not dealt with to the detriment of all involved.

The tyranny of being perfect haunts too many people. To learn that making mistakes is normal and okay would be a marvelous present under every person's Christmas tree!

Systems want to remain the same. Systems resist change even if the change is beneficial. When the Explorer is invited to move in a sculpt to get what he or she needs and the other role players are told to follow what their insides say to them, the initial reaction usually is to resist the new movements of the Explorer. To paraphrase the old adage, "The devil you know is better than the angel you don't know." Since the system's energy is to remain with the familiar, the weaker members will find it nearly impossible to change things for the better. This is why I deal with the strongest member of a family or the one in most pain to bring about change. Ironically, this often happens to be one of the children.

One of the most frequent resistances I encounter in family reconstruction is toward the end of the day, when the Explorer has seen enough new pictures that the emotional network built up around the old pictures begins to be shattered. When this occurs the Explorer's self-identity is being challenged. One's self-identity is built on early perceptions and resulting feelings, especially those toward one's parents. If a person perceives his or her parents as always being critical, then that person sees himself or herself as a failure with all the feelings attendant upon being a failure. If an Explorer begins to see the parents in a new light (for example, understanding that they are critical because it is too threatening for them to have a child who fails), then the Explorer begins to get new feelings for the parents. Empathy, compassion and softness emerge. The shift in feelings and self-identity begins. However, even though it would seem better not to see oneself as a failure, the Explorer might begin to resist this shift. The Explorer prefers to maintain his or her self-identity as a failure rather than see oneself as normal and successful. The loss of one's old self-identity is very threatening! One has lived with it many years and has established a whole world view around it. To change it is to change one's world.

A person is in a very real sense all of one's family and not just the person circumscribed by the boundaries of his or her skin. By this I don't mean merely that a person receives his or her critical learnings from his or her family as described in Chapter 2. There is another level on which a person is one's family.

Let us fantasize the impossible ideal of a person becoming so autonomous that every learning, every meaning, every way of behaving, every rule within his or her psyche, every coping mechanism has been freely chosen. No unconscious mechanism functions within the person that was learned or borrowed from his parents. As a result, this "ideal" autonomous person is completely his own. The person can claim, "Nothing in me is caused by another, except my genes. I have freely chosen all else and have made it completely my own." This person on some ontological level is *still* his family—in fact, if he denied or ignored any of his family he would experience a certain sense of being incomplete.

For this reason it is dysfunctional for people to "cut off the parents" as a way to cope. For example, I recently talked to a woman who said that for years she has had to keep herself separate, cut off from her folks. When she tried to understand them deeply and feel some empathy and compassion for them, she experienced herself being "wiped out again"—as if she were enmeshed with them. She had to go back to her hardness and anger to keep her distance and boundaries, to be herself.

I suggested to her that her parents were acting badly toward her because in some way they were threatened. She agreed to that—in fact this is what she had come to see and to feel for them—and that led to her being "wiped out again." I then said that what she perhaps hadn't seen is a way her folks could have acted differently to cope with their threat other than "beating up on her" and that she had not seen a way to deal with her parents other than by separation.

Her eyes lifted and she smiled as if to say, "I had never thought of that," as if indeed there may be some truth to what I was saying that might allow her to embrace her parents in a new way and to allow her to be truly herself. She had felt the incompleteness of cutting off her parents as a way to protect herself. There was something deep inside that told her she would never be whole until she could accept her family.

The point I'm making is dramatically illustrated in the case of a baby adopted in the first week of its life. The learnings, except for the nine months in the womb and the one week with the biological mother, all come from the adopted parents. Yet adopted persons feel so much more complete after reconstructing both their biological parents and their adopted family. In some sense a person is more than himself; a person is also his or her family.

In order to help people quickly I go immediately to the rule of survival. This is best understood if we consider the following case: Martin came to me shaken and confused about his relationship with his wife, Barbara. He was feeling at his wits' end, fearing the relationship would not change and would end in divorce. He told me how upset he gets with his wife's anger, feeling unable to control it and her.

I asked him what happens to him when he encounters Barbara's anger. He told me he feels both blamed and scared. He is scared because he thinks the anger is going to get out of control and there will be violence inflicted upon him (which has happened at times). When he feels blamed he becomes defensive and blames her back. He insists Barbara examine her inner dynamics that cause such outbursts of anger ("If it weren't for you, I'd be okay"). Naturally, Barbara feels the blame coming from Martin and only gets more angry—to the point of violence at times. This repetitive pattern accomplishes nothing except to increase his despair about the future with his wife.

I asked Martin how he feels about being blamed by Barbara. He said he felt stunned and angry. I then asked, "How do you feel about feeling angry?" He replied, "I feel helpless." "And do you feel anything about feeling helpless?" "I feel desperate, panic-stricken."

I asked him to close his eyes and picture himself as a youngster growing up in his home. "Pick a scene in which you are helpless," I said. "You fail at something, can't do it right. See what happens."

After a long time, his mouth quivered, tears came, and his jaw set tight. He opened his eyes and said he came to a scene in which he was five years old and his mother told him to sweep the kitchen floor. He did, but she came in and angrily jerked the broom from his hands, pointing out all the dirt he had missed. She told him he'd never learn to do anything right. He felt crushed and absolutely worthless. He withdrew and determined he would never be a failure. All his life he was competitive and excelled in all areas he had particular talents for, but he assiduously avoided any ventures in which he might fail. Today he is a successful businessman yet failing to embark on small ventures that any teenager could accomplish. From his childhood he learned he would not survive if he ever failed, was helpless, or out of control. He coped by making sure he was always right and denying whatever failures he committed.

In this story we have the basic ingredients that are seen when a person is having difficulty dealing with some aspect of life. I will diagram it:

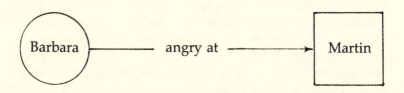

I. Martin puts a *meaning* on the anger ("I am being told I am wrong") and feels blamed.
II. From this *meaning* Martin *feels*:
   A. Stunned
   B. Angry
   C. Helpless
   D. Desperate, panicky—which is a tip-off that survival is at stake, therefore the "threatened" feeling
III. Martin's *rule of survival* is functioning: "If you fail I (mother) won't love you," which is interpreted unconsciously by Martin to mean "I'll die."

IV. Martin *protects* himself from the threat of not surviving. (To Barbara he says, "See what's wrong with you that you get so angry," blaming her while really saying to himself, "I'm not a failure, I'm not wrong—she is.")

Since Martin's basic coping mechanism (his stance in life) is never to be wrong, he must naturally deny any failure. He learned to do this by blaming. The coping mechanism is obviously dysfunctional.

This outline shows the four universal elements in any seriously dysfunctional behavior. Three of the four elements are learned: the meaning one assigns to an event, the rule of survival, and the way to cope in order to survive. By understanding this mechanism I have found myself going quickly to the heart of people's difficulties in order to help them.

Let me put it another way: Whenever a person comes to me wanting help I immediately suspect the dysfunctional behavior is a way of coping with being threatened. I must go to how the person is threatened, as that is the heart of the issue. I know that the interpretation the person has of the event stirs up the feelings. The feelings about the initial event tell me if a rule of survival is operating, so I then examine the feelings. I also know that, except for the feelings, all of this is learned in childhood, so I go to the source of the learning.

This mechanism allows several entry points to bring about help. I can deal with the meaning part of it, the coping part of it, or the rule of survival. Throughout this book various examples show entry at these different places. Family reconstruction deals with all three in a most powerful way.

Family reconstruction reveals repeatedly that, while under anger there is often a hurt feeling, the most pervasive feeling is one of helplessness. Recently, while teaching a class to people who were all involved in the throes of divorce, I asked the members to think of the recent times when they were angry and under that anger they did not also feel helpless. Not one person could think of a time when a sense of being powerless was not under the anger!

So in helping people deal with their anger, I help them gain some sense of power. As they move from feeling helpless, their anger diminishes. Often this involves seeing the situation in a different light and finding ways of having power other than trying harder to do what they had been doing in the past.

An example of this is the case of Jeff, a man whose wife left him for another man. He wanted to be rid of his anger. He was angry at her, and under the anger he felt rejected, hurt and helpless. He had only the faintest idea about all the different ways he felt helpless. I helped him discover that he felt helpless about doing anything about his loneliness and about his inability to care for himself in certain areas such as cooking and household chores. He also felt helpless in feeling that he was okay. The divorce was a blow to his pride, his manhood, and his ability to woo a woman and keep her attached to him.

Jeff would say things like, "What's wrong with me?" and "I'm no good." He felt wiped out and powerless. He had low self-esteem. He was so devastated that his problem-solving capacities, his imagination and his creativity were not functioning. His anger pushed his energies in only one direction—to regain his wife. This only drove her further away. Even when his divorce became final, he continued unconsciously to pursue his marriage by denying the divorce on some deep level and by hoping that the marriage would miraculously be restored. He was indeed stuck.

Rather than dealing directly with the anger, I helped Jeff deal with his helplessness. Gradually he found he could take care of his daily needs. After two months he even enrolled in a cooking school and began to make new friends. His sense of helplessness began to dissipate. He employed a housecleaner, who came in weekly. I then concentrated on helping him become aware of his other values as a human being. He soon found that a woman in his cooking class was attracted to him. He began to feel that he was not so worthless as a man after all. His sense of powerlessness began to vanish, and his anger toward his ex-wife diminished in direct proportion to the revitalization of his sense of power.

Realizing how helplessness is under anger enabled me to help another man who was living in fear that his divorced wife was so angry at him she might literally kill him. I helped him see what his wife felt so helpless about. On a superficial level she felt helpless in simply surviving financially. Under that was a helplessness of never being able to get a decent job, as she felt worthless about her talents—and thus she felt helpless about feeling better about herself.

After realizing this, the man rearranged the financial settlement in such a way that she knew that until her death she would get an income from an independent bank trust. Her former husband had no control over that bank trust. Gradually she began to feel less helpless, and her anger subsided. Today she earns $30,000 a year and has a civil relationship with her former husband.

Family reconstruction uncovers the pervasive need for people to change their parents rather than themselves. Many people will acknowledge that the real issue is the self, but as a family reconstruction unfolds you will often notice how the Explorer unconsciously slips into an effort to change his or her parents. The effort to get parents to understand and accept the Explorer is the way this demand for change manifests itself. This, of course, is quite natural, for as children we needed our parents not only to love and care for us but also to understand and accept us.

This subtle demand for parents to change rather than for self to change doesn't manifest itself as clearly in one-to-one therapy; nevertheless it can be present and absorb a great deal of energy from the client that could be better used to change the self. Behind so much effort for others to change is a hidden blame, "If it weren't for you, I'd be happy."

Often the characteristics of the Explorer are the characteristics of the family system. If the Explorer is open or closed, into denial or honesty, angry or composed, despondent or joyful, so the system will be open or closed, into denial or honesty, etc. A good example of this is the family of an alcoholic. As the alcoholic is denying, so will the family. One reason for this is that a child growing up in such a system learns the rules of behavior from the system. Another reason is that a person, for example one who denies painful reality, tends to marry someone with the same tendency so there can be mutual support for denying. Then the two denying spouses form the system that produces children who learn to deny. This does not always hold true. Some members of a system may reject the overriding rule of the system. Each person has that marvelous opportunity of being free and different, even though it may be difficult to buck the system.

The issue of integrating the various parts of one's personality is a common need. Playfulness needs to be integrated with seriousness, mildness with strength, being loose and relaxed with being responsible, the affective part with the intellectual part. This integration is a basic developmental problem that faces all of us.

I have discovered that when a person has a problem integrating apparent opposites (such as flexibility with assertiveness), often that person's parents represented the two poles and they never integrated those traits in their relationship. The father may have been very flexible and compromising, while the mother was very assertive and rigid. In the relationship the father failed to integrate assertiveness into his personality and the mother failed to integrate flexibility with her assertiveness. They relied on the other to supply that quality for them: "I don't need to make any decisions; your mother will do that."

Even though what partially draws people together in marriage is that one has what the other hasn't, it should not remain that way forever. The relationship offers the opportunity for each to learn from the other so that each can incorporate what is lacking into his or her own personality. When that is *not* done—when mother or father lean on the other to provide that trait throughout their marriage—then the child of such a union will have difficulty integrating the opposite parts within his or her personality. (The marriage, too, will be in jeopardy.)

When the parents do learn from each other and grow in the effort to integrate their own parts, then the child has a model of how to do that. Those coming from such families have less difficulty integrating opposites within themselves.

Family reconstruction reveals how often the anger toward one parent is more often a displaced anger toward the other parent. For example, a son may be very angry at his father for the cruel, harsh and rigidly controlling way he is treated by his father. The son feels no anger at all toward the mother; in fact, the mother has been his safe harbor. During family reconstruction what often emerges is that the Explorer gets in touch for the first time with years of buried and hidden anger toward his mother for not intervening, for not confronting the father regarding his cruel behavior. The young son could never dare allow himself to be angry at both parents simultaneously. To risk losing one parent (by being angry at the parent) is bad enough; to risk losing both is intolerable to a small child who needs at least one parent for survival.

During the family reconstruction the Explorer not only uncovers this hidden anger but also comes to understand why the mother did not intervene. She herself may have been too intimidated by her husband's rage. She may have felt that being a safe harbor for her son was a sufficient way to cope with the dilemma.

At times the displaced anger can be directed at a sibling. Because showing anger and frustration at one's parents is too risky, a child will be angry at a brother or sister. This is safer and allows the discharge of the anger.

Being aware of this tendency to displace anger helps me to better understand and work with the anger in an Explorer or a client. If enormous amounts of energy are devoted to hiding anger, uncovering it may help eliminate blockages the client may be having in his or her current life.

The most difficult people to deal with in a family reconstruction are the super-reasonable types. They are like blocks of granite. No wonder others living intimately with them can get so frustrated and angry with them. Trying to arouse them is such a seemingly hopeless task, especially when they are threatened. They protect themselves by simply not feeling. They cut themselves off from others' feelings as well. To have practically every member of a family be super-reasonable is the toughest system to crack. Such family reconstructions tend to be deadly dull—there are no feelings, there is no life! The slightest arousal of feeling may be an enormous step forward for a super-reasonable person—and it could be a very draining experience for such a person, even though outwardly it doesn't appear to be.

I have come to observe that recovering alcoholics and other chemically addicted persons are especially vulnerable people. It is not that their families of origin provided such painful environments—other people can have equally painful family experiences—but rather, it seems that while in the state of addiction these persons' *emotional* lives were at a standstill. The drugs anesthetize the sensitivities of the addict's emotional system. Thus, the chemically dependent person does not learn how to deal with feelings the way a nondrugged person does.

A teenager normally experiences powerful feelings of sexuality, idealism, romance, guilt, hero worship, confusion, hurt, betrayal, inferiority, insecurity. The teenager struggles to handle those feelings and in the process matures and becomes stronger. A teenager on drugs does not contend with those sharp and powerful feelings because of being desensitized. The recovering chemically dependent person, being arrested in his or her emotional development, is at the emotional stage he was at when entering into drug dependency. A 25-year-old recovering alcoholic, who became dependent at the age of 15, has the emotional maturity of a 15-year-old. This emotional immaturity makes recovering chemically dependent people especially vulnerable.

Family reconstruction has taught me how omnipresent and powerful stereotyping is. Once I was collaborating in a month-long residential training program in family therapy. I was co-leading with two other colleagues. At the end, when we were saying our goodbyes, a participant came up to me and with tremendous anger accused me of not supporting one of the co-leaders during the month. We were all shocked to hear this, especially the co-leader whom I had allegedly not supported. One of the leaders invited this woman to close her eyes and see if I reminded her of anyone in her past. In a moment she began to cry vehemently. After she subsided she opened her eyes and said that I resembled her father, who had consistently abandoned her mother. She was furious at her father. I reminded her of her father and received the brunt of the anger. For an entire month she had not been able to see me as a separate person different from her father.

So powerful is the contamination that can result from such stereotyping that often, in the beginning of a seminar or class, I'll ask the participants to close their eyes to see if I remind them of anyone in their past. I ask them to recall what their feelings were toward that person, positive or negative, and if those feelings have anything to do with how they are feeling toward me now. An average of from 30 to 45 percent of a group will admit to this phenomenon, and that indeed their feelings toward me are influenced by the person I resemble. Once a person becomes aware of doing this he or she can make a conscious effort to make the separation.

How often a spouse puts the face of mother or father on the marital partner. But once the tendency to do this comes into awareness, the person is able to deal with the real partner rather than with the stereotype.

The threat of nuclear war has added a new dimension to the psychological existence of people. A family came to me in which the 15-year-old girl was having problems in school. The conscientious parents were concerned that there might be more to the symptom than just a temporary snag with studies and teachers. As we got into the therapy, we discovered some relational issues that were disturbing the girl. We brought some successful resolution to the disturbances. Toward the end of several hours of work, I summarized our insights, decisions, resolutions and behavior. Then the girl said there was one more thing left out: She was having difficulty planning her future and was getting no help from anyone.

A light went on in my head. I remembered the research on children and nuclear weapons. Over 50 percent believe they will be in a nuclear war and will not survive. I told the girl that I wanted to ask a question that might not seem relevant to what we had been dealing with during our sessions, but that I wanted her to take her time and answer as honestly as she could. I then asked, "Dorothy, do you believe you will be in a nuclear war before you are an adult?"

She remained silent for what seemed a long time and then looked up at me and said, "Yes."

"Do you believe you will survive?"

"No," she said.

"No wonder you are having difficulties with your future!" I replied.

I turned toward the parents. There was a blank stare in

the father's eyes betraying a hopeless confusion. The mother's face showed fear. I asked them their reaction to what they heard. The mother gasped and said her stomach was in her throat. "What can I do or say?" she asked. "I can't do anything about that. I feel so scared and helpless."

The father in a monotone voice said that during the Cuban missile crisis when he was in the service he believed he would die in a nuclear war, but that belief vanished after a year or two. His voice trailed off as he was saying this, indicating he had no solution for his daughter.

I told them that I feel the same helplessness to an extent, but that I waver back and forth from helplessness and despair to hope and action. "I don't know if this will help you or not," I said, "but what I have to say helps me in the face of this overwhelming dilemma. First of all, I hope even in the face of the apparent hopelessness of the situation. There is not much reason for the hope, but in some mysterious way I still hope that we will be spared such an end to the world. Then I do what little I can and do believe in, such as support the nuclear freeze, write letters, vote for politicians who are not hawks, join SANE, read books like Ken Keyes' *The Hundredth Moneky*[1] and Freeman Dyson's *Weapons and Hope*.[2]

"Perhaps, most of all I am sustained by the conviction that eliminating nuclear weapons is not the major concern. What threatens nations so much that they need those weapons to 'protect' themselves? Whatever the content of the threat (communism, losing one's way of life), under that is fear. Fear is an energy out there in the universe as well as in the bodies of people. And love is an energy that dispels fear.

"As love increases within people and in the universe, fear is conquered. So I try to increase my own capacity to love.

[1]Vision Books, 1982.
[2]Harper & Row, 1984.

As I help you eliminate your family wars and help you love more in your family, I believe we are adding in some small way to the increment of love in the universe. As this love builds up, the fear of being threatened diminishes. Thus, the need for nuclear defense might someday vanish. This belief supports my hope and encourages the need to love all the more, adding to my purpose in doing therapy and family reconstructions. As I see you going home and loving each other, I have hope for our future."

I felt some relief in my office as I finished my little talk. I must add that I think the specter of a nuclear war destroying mankind is infinitely more disturbing than the specter of one's personal death. Deep in our collective unconscious (or whatever is akin to that within us) is the knowledge that, while indeed we die, we also live on in some way—through our children, our good works in society, reincarnation, immortality or whatever. The end of all life on this planet has an air of finality to it that is not present in individual dying. This is why the presence of nuclear weapons today has truly added a new dimension to the psychological existence of each person on the earth.

People need a meaning, purpose or commitment beyond themselves. Sometimes I see people in therapy who are unhappy simply because they have no goals in life besides living for themselves. The root of their problem is not some psychological blockage, or a lack of skills, or an unresolved problem with their family of origin. They are restless and unfulfilled because in trying to become self-fulfilled and self-enlightened, they have made themselves their own goal in life. A part of them is undeveloped. They need to live for more than just themselves. They need to give themselves to others and to a higher realm of reality. That dimension of life commonly called the spiritual or religious sphere of existence seems to be nonexistent.

I tell these unfulfilled clients that I doubt if they will ever be satisfied until they become truly generous and committed to something or someone beyond themselves. I think they need spiritual awakening—not therapy. I can sympathize with many being turned off by previous experiences with certain rigidities and doctrinaire tenets of religion. I can also understand many rejecting the institutionalization of religion that stifles the spirit of religion. Still, I believe these people need an authentic experience that taps into that part of themselves that offers them meaning, purpose and commitment beyond themselves.

The underdeveloped side of a personality has difficulty flourishing in a marriage. One of the most subtle dysfunctional aspects of marriage is how polarities begin to function outside of the awareness of the couple involved. This hinders the development of the full personality. For example, the wife may be very gentle and warm while the husband is tough, demanding, and able to hold the line. A developed personality has both sets of traits; both are needed for a fully functioning life.

Often a man is attracted to a woman because he sees in her those traits that are not developed in himself, and vice versa. So their coupling begins. However, as their relationship grows the polarity can set in, i.e., the woman becomes more gentle and less tough while the man becomes more tough and less gentle. Outwardly it looks as if they are just depending on the other to provide those traits in the marriage. However, I believe the polarity grows from deeper, more subtle sources, most of the time sources unconscious to each of them.

The husband, for example, may be afraid of his gentleness; it may weaken his ability to hold the line. Not expressing his gentleness often, he is not at home with it. Add to this the fact that his wife is warm and gentle; in her this quality has been well developed. So when the occasion demands gentleness, the wife responds quickly and easily. The husband, being less adept at being gentle, sees the field being preempted by his wife. He feels slightly jealous, and perhaps like a failure. When he sees that his wife's gentleness needs to be strengthened by some toughness, he steps in to supply that. He can quickly and easily do this since he is more adept at being tough and strong. Then the wife may feel jealous and like a failure, thus pulling her strength back in.

All this happens at such a deep level that neither may be aware of the feelings of jealousy and failure. Then each can begin to resent the other for preempting the field, as it were. Resentment grows in the husband as he feels more and more helpless to express his gentleness, so he retrenches into what he does best, i.e., show strength. As this pattern of behavior grows, the wife's gentleness becomes so one-sided that it forces the husband to be even stronger, while the husband's toughness forces the wife to be adamantly gentle. Soon an almost unbreakable polarity is established.

This pattern can be broken if the husband and wife have sufficient time and space apart. In their separateness, the husband can find the room to let his gentleness out and the wife has room to allow her toughness to emerge. I see this so often as a major issue in marriage that I am convinced a healthy marriage demands plenty of separation for the husband and wife. Too often each partner feels guilty when separated—unless there is a justifiable reason, such as business endeavors. However, separation is needed just for the sake of separation.

Unfortunately, for many only a permanent separation allows each to develop the underdeveloped side of his or her personality because the polarity has become so locked in. The existence of such polarities is extremely stressful for both partners, since one is never balanced and constantly needs to be rescued, while in reality the underdeveloped side cries out for life of its own within each person.

Helping people become whole and functional is at least in theory as simple as enlarging their reality. In family reconstruction, the Explorer is encouraged to identify with the new pictures and experiences emerging in the drama. Frequent questions put to the Explorer are, "Do you know anything about that?" "Have you ever felt that way?" "Have you ever done anything like that?" As the Explorer identifies his or her own experiences with that of mother, father or siblings, then at that point a new map of reality enters the Explorer. The new mother and father are added to the old mother and father within the Explorer. In the very process of adding these new realities, the old dysfunctional dynamics and patterns vanish. At that precise moment, that which was dysfunctional becomes functional.

For example, in Ann's reconstruction (described in Chapters 6 and 7), we saw how Ann's attitude toward her mother changed. Ann not only *saw* how her mother as a child was confused and never asserted herself, but could reach down into her own experiences and *identify* with her mother's experience of being confused and non-assertive. The identification allowed Ann to take in her mother in a new way. A new map of reality was added to Ann. At that point the old dysfunctional way of viewing and dealing with mother was transformed. The old way Ann dealt with her mother was dysfunctional because a piece of reality was missing. Ann was missing a piece of understanding mother's confusion and helplessness.

The more I think about it, the more it appears to me that any dysfunctional transaction, behavior or pattern lacks a piece of reality. If I am depressed I ignore the positive attributes that are mine. If I am lonely, I fail to recognize my potential for communication and relating as well as the need that others have for connecting. If I blame I am disregarding the other person's thoughts, feelings and needs. If I stay in obstinate disagreement I am missing the value of the other's position.

If this is true, then becoming functional means simply adding to one's reality. Helping others become whole and functional means helping them add to their reality. So perhaps all that is needed to help people is to add what is missing. The artistry of doing that is the art of therapy or of any helping relationship.

* * *

These are some of the lessons that have carved themselves into my mind over the years, as I have led family reconstructions, as well as dealt with people in private therapy. As I mentioned earlier, I have learned more about family systems doing family reconstruction than from any other single source. Family reconstruction puts the issues and problems talked about in one-to-one therapy into the liveliness of drama. Thus, the lessons are easier to see and etched more deeply in my mind.

EPILOGUE

Virginia Satir in her book *Peoplemaking* sums up a nurturing or functional family: "In . . . nurturing families I consistently see . . . self-worth is high; communication is direct, clear, specific and honest; rules are flexible, human, appropriate, and subject to change; and the linking to society is open and hopeful."[1]

The sign that a system is functional rather than dysfunctional is simply how good the members of that system feel about themselves. If they feel good about themselves, feel fully alive, are expressive and creative with a sense of joy and peace and freedom, then the bets are on that they live in a nurturing family or system. Such a nurturing system does not fall out of the sky; it is not instinctually natural. Such a system results from knowing and applying the necessary processes and ingredients. It takes study, disciplined effort and a graciousness to learn from the mistakes made along the way.

One of the most important aspects of a nurturing and functional system is how threats are dealt with in the system. I am particularly pleased by what I have written about the congruent way to deal with threat. This way tends to diminish the threat itself!

Any program of training, teaching, inner discipline, system of thought or religion, process (including family recon-

[1]Virginia Satir, *Peoplemaking* (Palo Alto, CA: Science and Behavior Books, Inc., 1972 edition), p. 4.

struction) that helps people deal with threats in a way that diminishes the threat itself needs to be supported and expanded. This is especially so in face of the threat of nuclear annihilation. Since all of us learn how to deal with threat from within our family of origin, family reconstruction is a particularly powerful tool to help people transform dysfunctional coping mechanisms into the functional one of being congruent.

Within family reconstructions, dealing congruently with threat leads to the shedding of hard, angry, hateful feelings and replacing those feelings with attitudes of understanding, forgiveness, reconciliation and love. Through family reconstruction, participants learn to live and let live; they quit trying to force change in others and take good care of themselves in the process. As a result there is room for two to live without one coercing or destroying or threatening the other. And when we can do this with the most powerful people threatening us (a mother or father), then a way is learned to do it with less powerful people. As each person learns to cope with threat in a non-threatening way (i.e., congruently), then there is hope that this coping mechanism will be used in the larger systems of social, political, economic, cultural and international life. So it pleases me to know that this book and the greater usage of family reconstruction will add to the cause of peace in the world.

APPENDIX:
A DO-IT-YOURSELF
FAMILY RECONSTRUCTION

It is my conviction that there is nothing as powerful as a live family reconstruction whereby a Guide leads the process with an Explorer and a group of role players. The Explorer experiences his or her family members expressing their thoughts and feelings and, perhaps for the first time, communicating openly and honestly. The Explorer sees what might have happened if the family members had had the courage to go after what they needed. In this live reconstruction the Explorer is thrust into the action and has new experiences with family members: speaking honestly as never before, breaking dysfunctional rules, absorbing new meanings, expressing feelings previously suppressed. However, since it is not always possible to do a live family reconstruction, I have added this appendix.

I have seen great changes occur in people when they simply do the work described in Chapter 3, "The Explorer Gathers the Supplies." I have seen changes in others from just reading the manuscript of this book. For this reason I have drafted and tested the following series of exercises that will enable you to have a "do-it-yourself" family reconstruction. I feel assured that you will gain immensely from this experience and that you will be encouraged to do your live family reconstruction. Even if you are not aware of any current dilemmas in your life, doing these exercises will fill out wholeness and well-being. Something invisibly, mysteriously and unconsciously occurs simply in the process of doing a reconstruction, even if there is no major issue facing the Explorer.

The process of family reconstruction has always added a wealth of awarenesses that were previously hidden. It adds roots to one's life. As the TV series "Roots" was so rewarding for so many people because it tapped into the psychological hunger for knowing one's roots, so family reconstruction does the same. We are more than just what is circumscribed by our skin. We are part of a whole tree going back to our parents' families and, less overtly, beyond that. As you stand before a mirror, you are not just what you see. You are all those invisible people standing beside you, your brothers and sisters; behind you, your parents and aunts and uncles; and behind them, your grandparents. You are part of a huge tree with deep roots, and when you become more fully aware of your roots you are actualizing your entire being. Even when the distorted part of that tree (for example, a child beater or an alcoholic) is brought into the open, it still adds to your wholeness.

I encourage you to embark upon your own journey now. Be an adventurous Explorer, making the strenuous effort and taking the necessary time to do these step-by-step exercises. At the end of the journey you will come into a light previously hidden.

Before you begin this work I suggest that you do this with a trusting friend, relative or spouse. This way you will have someone to share your work with and they with you, thereby relieving the burden of the length and the depth of the work. It will stimulate you to further insights and give you the rich opportunity to share your feelings with someone who cares.

1) Complete the work described in Chapter 3, "The Explorer Gathers His Supplies." This will take some 10 to 20 hours.

Be sure to write down your feelings and reactions after doing each of the four segments. Throughout these exercises,
whenever you do not know the facts or reality, simply fantasize and make up or guess the reality.

2) As you move from exercise to exercise keep a diary. Record
the reactions stirred up in you as a result of this work.

3) Put your three family maps or genograms on three separate
large pieces of paper or poster board, leaving plenty of space
to write in other data. Under each name, list all of the adjectives and traits that describe that person. Be sure to list
both positive and negative traits. For example, see Figure 22.

After you list all the adjectives, study the three maps asking
yourself the following questions:

A. Who resembles whom in these families?
B. Whom do I resemble? What qualities do I have from whom?
C. Examine the three marital relationships. What draws the spouses
together?
D. What patterns do I see?
E. What patterns am I replicating in my life?
F. How do the people I resemble handle their strengths and weak-
nesses? How do I handle mine?
G. How am I different from those I resemble?
H. How does my loved one or spouse resemble any members of
my family?
I. What draws me to my significant other, and vice versa?

When you finish this exercise, write down your reactions.

4) On sufficiently large pieces of paper, lay out each family to
demonstrate how the family members relate to each other.
Do your paternal and maternal families first. Draw lines and
write words to describe how they related to each other, or
write simple sentences that would state the basic message
each would give to the other. Then put words under each

Family Reconstruction

Figure 22.

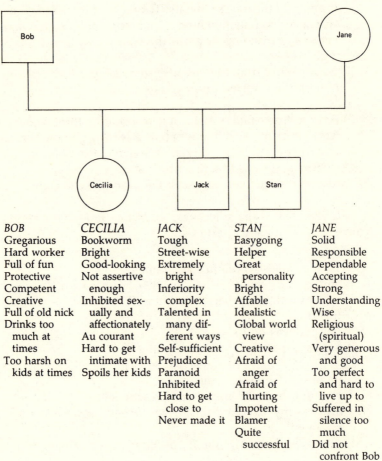

BOB	CECILIA	JACK	STAN	JANE
Gregarious	Bookworm	Tough	Easygoing	Solid
Hard worker	Bright	Street-wise	Helper	Responsible
Full of fun	Good-looking	Extremely	Great	Dependable
Protective	Not assertive	bright	personality	Accepting
Competent	enough	Inferiority	Bright	Strong
Creative	Inhibited sex-	complex	Affable	Understanding
Full of old nick	ually and	Talented in	Idealistic	Wise
Drinks too	affectionately	many dif-	Global world	Religious
much at	Au courant	ferent ways	view	(spiritual)
times	Hard to get	Self-sufficient	Creative	Very generous
Too harsh on	intimate with	Prejudiced	Afraid of	and good
kids at times	Spoils her kids	Paranoid	anger	Too perfect
		Inhibited	Afraid of	and hard to
		Hard to get	hurting	live up to
		close to	Impotent	Suffered in
		Never made it	Blamer	silence too
			Quite	much
			successful	Did not
				confront Bob
				enough

name describing the basic feeling each felt due to their being in the family. After reflecting on your work, ask yourself,
"What do I learn concerning myself from all this?" Write
down your reflections. For example, see Figure 23.

Stan, the Explorer in Figure 23, writes his reactions:

They were all doing the best they knew. I never realized how much pain was there. Yet there was a sense of life and a joy of life, laughter, partying. Mother had enormous strength and wanted ever so much to be loved with affection, yet I wonder if she could give it to an equal? I think she got caught up in old fear of being abandoned when Father began to fail. She couldn't cope

Figure 23.

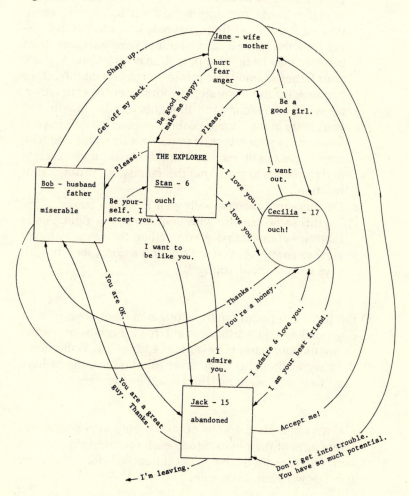

except by being strong and taking over. I must never let fear traumatize me into having only one way to react. I'm grateful I have the best of both parents in me and have had since I was 20 years of age. I need to be as accepting of Jack now as I used to be, yet strong enough to care for my own needs.

5) a) Close your eyes and imagine a sculpture of the family of your father as illustrated by the pictures in Chapter 6. Let your fantasy be as detailed as possible. Imagine the color of the clothes, furniture in the room, facial expressions, time of the day. At first what may occur to you is hearing something like a family fight or family singing, then pictures may begin to appear. It may be helpful to place your father's family tree before you as you do this. Once you imagine the sculpture, in your fantasy be your father, allowing his feelings and thoughts to arise in you. Put your body in the precise position of your father's in your fantasy. As your father, express your thoughts and feelings to his family members and fantasize their reaction and responses to you. After this fantasy, write down your reaction.
   b) Do this same exercise with your mother's family.
   c) Do this same exercise with your family of origin. Again fantasize yourself first as your father, then as your mother, then as you. As you write your reactions, see what this says to you about yourself.

6) Put the map of your family of origin in front of you. Write down what you surmise might have been some secret thoughts your parents never told each other. Write down their secret thoughts they never told you but might have liked to if they were not threatened in some way.

7) Gather some photographs of your family members at different ages of their lives. Study each one carefully to see if you recognize anything you never noticed before. If you do, write down your discoveries.

8) a) After a day or so, reread your writings in your manual and recall your fantasies and images. Placing a picture of your mother before you, write her a letter expressing all you want to her. This letter is not to be sent to her if she is still alive. Later on you may wish to write a new letter and send it to her.

 b) Do the same with your father.

 c) Read the following instructions only after you have written your two letters: Be your father and write a letter in response to yours. Be your mother and write a letter in response to yours.

9) As you look back at your life, during which two or three time spans did you feel most alive? (For example, it may have been your first year away at college or during your first pregnancy.) During which two or three events did you feel most alive? (For example, it may have been the time you made your highest mountain climb, or while giving birth to your first child, or after landing your biggest business deal.)

After you identify the two or three time spans and two or three events, analyze each of them to see what gave you this great sense of being fully alive.

With this information in hand, imagine what you could do in the next year to have that same sense of being fully alive. Imagine it for the next five years.

10) On a sheet of paper, list five or six of your most salient positive characteristics and several of your most predominant negative traits. Opposite to each indicate the negative and positive seeds buried in each. It is from these seeds that the traits can be transformed. For example:

Positive	*Seeds that could produce a negative characteristic*
Gregarious ⟶	boring
Strong ⟶	domineering
Sensitive ⟶	too easily hurt→fear of closeness
Bright ⟶	arrogant
Organized ⟶	rigid

Negative	*Seeds that could produce a positive characteristic*
Blaming ⟶	ability to be in touch with self and care for self
Lazy ⟶	relaxed, non-possessive
Absent-minded ⟶	total absorption or concentration

If you want to transform the negatives into the positives buried in them, take each one and write down what you need to do to bring that about.

BIBLIOGRAPHY

Family reconstruction blends Gestalt, hypnosis, fantasy, communications, body language, the unconscious and family systems theory into a marvelous whole. This explains how the following readings over the years have coalesced to help me in guiding family reconstructions.

Family Systems
Napier, A. & Whitaker, C. *The Family Crucible*. New York: Harper & Row, 1978.
Satir, Virginia. *Conjoint Family Therapy*. Palo Alto, CA: Science and Behavior Books, Inc., 1967.
Satir, Virginia. *Peoplemaking*. Palo Alto, CA: Science and Behavior Books, Inc., 1972.

Developmental Psychology
Jersild, A. T. *Child Psychology*. Englewood Cliffs, NJ: Prentice-Hall, 1960.
Jersild, A. T. *The Psychology of Adolescence*. New York: Macmillan, 1963.
Maslow, Abraham. *Toward a Psychology of Being*. New York: Van Nostrand-Reinhold Co., 1968.

Gestalt
Perls, F. *Gestalt Therapy Verbatim*. Lafayette, CA: Real People Press, 1969.
Perls, Fritz. *The Gestalt Approach and Eye Witness to Therapy*. Palo Alto: Science and Behavior Books, Inc., 1973.

Miscellaneous
Jersild, Arthur T. *When Teachers Face Themselves*. New York: Bureau of Publications, Teachers College, Columbia University, 1955.
Goffman, Erving. *Asylums*. New York: Anchor Books, 1961.

Three other books that don't quite fit into the above categories have greatly contributed to the way I think about and do family reconstruction: The first is the New Testament, the second is the collected writings of Martin Luther King, and the third is the human being. Once I asked a wise professor engaged in international diplomacy which books he deemed most important. He replied, "The human being is the most important book I ever read." It dawned on me years later that while the professor said it, my father first taught that lesson to me by his actions, as nothing so engaged him as another human being.

INDEX

DATE DUE